Food List Encyclopedia for Diabetes

The Complete Updated Guide of Foods that Don't Spike Blood Sugar to Stay Healthy All Year Round

Sarah Diomy

TABLE OF CONTENTS

GET ACCESS TO 1000+ DELICIOUS <u>DIABETIC-FRIENDLY</u> RECIPES

Recipes n. 384: Pork Chops Crusted in Almonds

(**Preparation time**: 10 minutes | **Cooking time:** 20 minutes | **Difficulty**: Easy | **Servings**: 2)

Ingredients:
- 1/2 cup of grated low-fat parmesan cheese
- 2 (3-4 oz.) of boneless pork chops
- 1/2 cup of almonds chopped finely
- 1/4 cup of Dijon mustard
-

Instructions:
- Preheat the oven at 400°F. Wrap foil around a baking tray.
- Place three bowls on the table. Scatter the remaining ingredients, including Dijon mustard, grated parmesan, & sliced almonds, on each plate.
- Apply a layer of mustard, then a layer of grated

cheese, and finally a layer of chopped almonds on one pork chop at a time. Spread the mixture out on a baking sheet.

- Bake for about 15 minutes. To avoid overcooking, check for an internal temperature of 140-145 °F. Serve with a veggie that isn't starchy.

Do you want to **get access** to the full list of <u>1000+ recipes </u>that can potentially **save** your health?

SCAN THE QR CODE
AND
GET <u>FREE</u> ACCESS →

Chapter 1: Understanding Diabetes

What exactly is Diabetes?

Diabetes is a long-term disease that impairs the body's capacity to handle glucose, generally known as blood sugar. Glucose is an important source of energy for the body's cells, notably those in the brain. The pancreas-produced hormone insulin is crucial in controlling the quantity of glucose in the circulation. It promotes the entrance of glucose into cells, where it is converted into energy. This system is disturbed in diabetes due to either inadequate insulin synthesis or the body's inability to utilize insulin efficiently, a condition known as insulin resistance. As a result, glucose accumulates in the bloodstream, resulting in hyperglycemia (high blood sugar). Persistent hyperglycemia can harm multiple organs over time, including the heart, kidneys, nerves, and eyes. Diabetes is classified into various categories, each with its own set of causes and treatments. Diabetes is classified into three types: **type 1, type 2, and gestational diabetes**.

Type 1 diabetes, also known as insulin-dependent diabetes or juvenile diabetes, is characterized by the immune system targeting and killing insulin-producing cells in the pancreas. This degradation results in an absolute insulin shortage.

Type 2 diabetes, formerly known as non-insulin-dependent or adult-onset diabetes, is caused by a combination of insulin resistance and the pancreas's failure to generate enough insulin to overcome this resistance. Obesity and a sedentary lifestyle are frequently associated with type 2 diabetes.

Gestational diabetes is a disorder that develops during pregnancy. Hormonal changes make the body's cells less receptive to insulin in this scenario. While gestational diabetes normally goes away once the baby is delivered, it increases the mother's chance of acquiring type 2 diabetes later in life. Other, less frequent kinds of diabetes include monogenic diabetes, a hereditary type of diabetes, and cystic fibrosis-related diabetes. Diabetes is a severe disease, but it is manageable with proper medical treatment and lifestyle adjustments. Diabetes therapy aims to keep blood sugar levels as near to normal as possible in order to avoid or reduce the onset of problems. These therapies involve a mix of medication or insulin therapy, dietary changes, frequent physical activity, and blood sugar monitoring. Understanding diabetes and its effects on the body is critical for people who have it. This comprehension enables more educated decision-making, better self-care habits, and improved communication with healthcare professionals.

Diabetes Types

Diabetes is classified into three types: type 1, type 2, and gestational diabetes. Each variety has its own process and features, but they all result in an increase in blood sugar levels.

Diabetes mellitus type 1

Type 1 diabetes, formerly known as juvenile diabetes, accounts for 5-10% of all diabetes cases. It is most commonly diagnosed in children, teenagers, and young adults, but it can happen at any age. This is an autoimmune disorder in which the body's immune system assaults and kills insulin-producing beta cells in the pancreas. As a result, there is a total or near-complete insulin insufficiency. The precise source of this autoimmune reaction is unknown, although it is thought to be a mix of genetic and environmental factors, probably viruses, that produce the condition. Type 1 diabetes symptoms might include excessive thirst, frequent urination, exhaustion, weight loss despite regular or increased eating, and impaired vision. Type 1 diabetics require insulin therapy for the rest of their lives. Insulin can be administered by many daily injections or through an insulin pump. Type 1 diabetes management also entails frequent blood sugar monitoring, a nutritious diet, and regular exercise.

Diabetes mellitus type 2

Type 2 diabetes is the most prevalent, accounting for approximately 90-95% of all diabetes occurrences. It is distinguished by insulin resistance, which occurs when the body's cells do not respond effectively to insulin and cannot efficiently absorb glucose from the blood. The pancreas adjusts in the early stages of type 2 diabetes by producing more insulin. However, with time, the pancreas cannot keep up with the demand, and insulin production may diminish. Obesity, sedentary lifestyle, poor nutrition, rising age, and a family history of diabetes are the key risk factors for type 2 diabetes. It is more frequent in adults, but it is becoming increasingly common in children and adolescents as childhood obesity rates rise. Because symptoms are generally milder than in type 1 diabetes and may go unnoticed, many persons with type 2 diabetes are unaware they have the condition until problems arise. Unlike type 1 diabetes, type 2 diabetes is frequently manageable by lifestyle modifications and oral drugs. As the condition worsens, insulin may be required.

Gestational Diabetes

Gestational diabetes develops throughout pregnancy, most commonly during the second or third trimester. During pregnancy, hormonal changes cause a woman's body to become less receptive to insulin, a condition known as insulin resistance. Most women's pancreas can compensate by producing extra insulin. However, this does not happen in all women, resulting in gestational diabetes. It normally goes away after childbirth, but it is dangerous to both the mother and the infant. Women who have gestational diabetes are more likely to have difficulties during pregnancy and delivery, and their children are more likely to develop obesity and type 2 diabetes later in life. Women who have gestational diabetes are more likely to acquire type 2 diabetes after giving birth. Diet, exercise, and, in certain situations, insulin treatment are used to treat gestational diabetes. It is also critical for women to be screened for diabetes following pregnancy. Understanding a person's type of diabetes is critical since it influences treatment strategy and gives insight into potential complications. It also emphasizes the significance of leading a healthy lifestyle in order to avoid or manage this chronic illness.

Risk Factors and Causes

Understanding the origins and risk factors of diabetes is critical for developing preventative and treatment methods. This awareness also enables individuals to adopt lifestyle changes that can have a substantial impact on the disease's progression.

Causes of Diabetes

The major cause of type 1 diabetes is an autoimmune reaction in which the body's immune system assaults insulin-producing cells in the pancreas. The precise cause of this autoimmune reaction is unknown, although it appears to include a mix of genetic predisposition and an environmental trigger, maybe a viral infection. Type 2 diabetes is caused by a mix of hereditary and environmental factors. Insulin resistance develops first, which means that the body's cells do not respond to insulin properly. To keep blood sugar levels under control, the pancreas produces more insulin. The pancreas eventually fails to keep up with the body's growing requirement for insulin, resulting in diabetes. Gestational diabetes is caused by hormonal changes during pregnancy that lead the cells in the body to utilize insulin inefficiently.

Diabetes Risk Factors

While the specific origin of diabetes is not always known, some risk factors enhance the chances of having the illness.

Risk factors for type 1 diabetes include:

- Family History: Having a parent or sibling with type 1 diabetes raises the risk, while the majority of persons with the condition have no family history.

- Genetics: Certain genes are associated with an increased chance of developing type 1 diabetes.
- Age: Type 1 diabetes often develops during infancy or adolescence, but it can occur at any age.

Risk factors for type 2 diabetes include:

- Being overweight or obese is a major risk factor. The more fatty tissue someone has, the more insulin resistant their cells become.
- Inactivity: Physical activity helps regulate weight, burns glucose for energy, and makes cells more insulin sensitive.
- A person's chance of developing type 2 diabetes increases if he or she has a parent or sibling who has the condition.
- Although type 2 diabetes can arise at any age, the risk rises with age, especially beyond the age of 45.
- Race or ethnicity: Certain ethnic groups, such as African Americans, Hispanics, American Indians, and Asian-Americans, are more prone than Caucasians to develop type 2 diabetes.
- Gestational Diabetes: Women who have experienced gestational diabetes are more likely to acquire type 2 diabetes later in life. Risk factors for gestational diabetes include:

Diagnosis and Symptoms

Diabetes must be detected early since quick diagnosis and treatment might avoid or postpone consequences. Understanding diabetes symptoms assists in early detection and medical intervention. Along with detecting symptoms, we'll go over how healthcare experts use several tests to diagnose diabetes.

Diabetes Symptoms

Diabetes symptoms are mostly caused by excessive blood glucose levels. While the appearance of these symptoms varies between diabetes types, frequent symptoms include:

- **Increased thirst and urination:** As excess sugar accumulates in the circulation, fluid is drawn from the tissues, resulting in increased thirst. This leads to increased drinking and urination.
- **Increased hunger:** Without enough insulin to transport sugar into cells, the muscles and organs lose energy, resulting in severe hunger.
- **Fatigue:** When a person's cells are deprived of sugar, he or she may become fatigued and angry.
- **Blurred vision:** High blood sugar levels can draw fluid from the lenses of the eyes, impairing focus. Diabetes impairs the body's capacity to heal and fight infections, resulting in slow-healing wounds or recurrent infections.
- **Weight loss that is unexplained:** Despite eating more than normal to satisfy hunger, one may lose weight. When the body is unable to digest glucose, it must rely on alternate fuels stored in muscle and fat. Calories are expended as extra glucose is excreted in the urine.

Symptoms of type 1 diabetes frequently appear fast and are more severe. Type 2 diabetes symptoms appear gradually and are subtler, which might cause a delay in diagnosis.

Diabetes Diagnosis

When diabetes is suspected based on symptoms, doctors often employ a battery of tests to confirm the diagnosis.

- A1C Test: This blood test offers information about a person's average blood glucose levels over the previous three months. Diabetes is diagnosed when the A1C result is 6.5 percent or greater on two different tests.

- **Fasting Blood Sugar Test** : A fasting blood sugar test is performed after an overnight fast. Normal fasting blood sugar levels are fewer than 100 milligrams per deciliter (mg/dL). A fasting blood sugar level of 100 to 125 mg/dL suggests prediabetes, whereas a result of 126 mg/dL or greater on two different tests implies diabetes.

- **Random Blood Sugar Test**: A blood sample is collected at random during a random blood sugar test. The blood sugar level is measured in milligrams per deciliter (mg/dL). Diabetes is indicated by a random blood sugar level of 200 mg/dL or above.

- **Oral Glucose Tolerance Test:** This test is often used to determine gestational diabetes during pregnancy. A person's blood sugar is tested after fasting. Then they consume a sweet beverage, and their blood sugar levels are checked every two hours for the following two hours. Normal blood sugar levels are fewer than 140 mg/dL. After two hours, a result of greater than 200 mg/dL suggests diabetes.

A healthcare professional may repeat a test on a separate day to confirm a diabetes diagnosis. It's also worth noting that even if a person doesn't have symptoms but has diabetes risk factors, routine tests should be done because early identification and treatment can avoid or delay consequences.

Chapter 2: Living With Type 1 Diabetes

An Overview of Type 1 Diabetes

Type 1 diabetes, also known as juvenile diabetes or insulin-dependent diabetes, is a chronic disease in which the pancreas produces very little or no insulin. It is a metabolic disorder—the way the body utilizes digested food for energy—caused mostly by an autoimmune reaction. We'll look at its etiology, signs & symptoms, treatment, and probable consequences. Diabetes

Pathophysiology Type 1

A dysfunction in the immune system lies at the heart of type 1 diabetes. The immune system, which is in charge of battling germs and viruses, mistakenly targets and kills insulin-producing beta cells in the pancreas. It is yet unknown what causes this autoimmune reaction. When a large number of beta cells are damaged, the body generates inadequate insulin, resulting in type 1 diabetes. Insulin is a hormone that permits cells to absorb glucose, a simple sugar, for energy production. Glucose cannot enter cells without insulin, thus it accumulates in the circulation, resulting in high blood sugar levels.

Type 1 Diabetes Signs and Symptoms

Type 1 diabetes symptoms can appear fast, in a matter of weeks, and can be severe in children and teenagers. They are as follows:

- **Frequent urination and thirst:** Excess sugar in the circulation causes fluid to be drawn from tissues. This causes thirst, which leads to increased drinking and urine.
- **Weight loss:** A person with type 1 diabetes may have unexplained weight loss while consuming more than normal. Because the body is unable to utilize glucose properly, it begins to burn fat and muscle for energy.

- **Wariness and weakness:** When cells are deprived of sugar, they become energy-starved, resulting in weariness.
- **Blurry vision:** High blood sugar levels can draw fluid from your eyes' lenses, impairing your ability to concentrate.

Managing of Type 1 Diabetes

Monitoring blood sugar levels and giving insulin are crucial to managing type 1 diabetes. This includes the following:

- **Insulin therapy:** Insulin treatment is required since the pancreas does not manufacture insulin in persons with type 1 diabetes. This can be administered by injections or an insulin pump.
- **Carbohydrate counting:** It is critical to understand how much carbohydrate is in meals and how it affects your blood sugar.
- **Frequent blood sugar monitoring:** It is vital to check blood sugar levels on a regular basis to ensure they are within the goal range recommended by the healthcare professional.
- **A balanced diet and regular physical activity**: A balanced diet and regular physical activity can assist to reduce blood sugar levels and manage weight.

Potential Type 1 Diabetes Complications

Type 1 diabetes, if not properly managed, can lead to major consequences such as heart disease, nerve damage, kidney damage, and eye damage. Individuals with this illness must have frequent check-ups and screenings to detect any possible consequences early. The first step toward optimal management of type 1 diabetes is to understand it. Individuals with type 1 diabetes may live healthy, active lives with the correct treatment plan, but it takes dedication and careful planning.

Type 1 Diabetes Management: Medication and Insulin Therapy

A diagnosis of type 1 diabetes frequently triggers a significant change in a person's life: a shift in their attitude to diet, activity, and general lifestyle. Effective type 1 diabetes treatment is a complicated but vital task that necessitates daily, if not hourly, blood sugar monitoring. Regular insulin treatment and, in certain situations, additional drugs are critical components of this management procedure. Understanding how these therapies operate can help people manage their condition more efficiently and reduce the likelihood of problems.

Insulin Therapy

Insulin treatment is a non-negotiable aspect of the daily routine for people with type 1 diabetes. Because the body generates little to no insulin, the hormone must be obtained from outside sources. This therapy seeks to be as near to the body's natural insulin production as feasible. There are several varieties of insulin, and they differ in terms of how soon they begin to function, when they peak, and how long they persist.

- Rapid-acting insulin begins to operate after 15 minutes of injection, peaks after one hour, and lasts for two to four hours.
- Short-acting insulin normally begins functioning within 30 minutes of injection, peaks two to three hours later, and continues to operate for three to six hours.
- Intermediate-acting insulin enters the bloodstream two to four hours after injection, peaks four to twelve hours later, and remains active for 12 to 18 hours.
- Long-acting insulin has the longest duration, reaching the circulation many hours after injection and lowering glucose levels for up to 24 hours or more.

Choosing the best type of insulin to use and the appropriate dosage is a joint choice made with a healthcare professional, taking into account aspects such as lifestyle, age, overall health, and the existence of any other medical disorders.

Insulin Delivery Methods

Traditionally, insulin is administered by injections with a small needle and syringe or an insulin pen – a pen-like device with a needle for a point. In recent years, however, technology has introduced a another way – the insulin pump. Insulin pumps provide a continuous supply of insulin rather than repeated injections. They provide quick or short-acting insulin through a catheter implanted under the skin 24 hours a day.

Additional Medications

Though insulin is the backbone of treatment, additional drugs are occasionally used in conjunction with insulin therapy to control type 1 diabetes. These may include drugs to control high blood pressure, cholesterol, and renal function.

Monitoring and Adjusting Treatment

Regular blood glucose monitoring is required for effective type 1 diabetes therapy. This daily duty is completed with the aid of a blood glucose meter, which delivers readings to assist you in making diet, exercise, and medication decisions. It is critical to remember that type 1 diabetes management is an ongoing process. Because a person's lifestyle, food, level of exercise, and even mental stress can all have an impact on blood glucose levels, the treatment plan, including the kind and amount of insulin administered, may need to be modified on a regular basis. To summarize, type 1 diabetes care focuses on striking a balance between insulin medication, food, and physical exercise to keep blood glucose levels within the desired range.

This is a lifelong commitment that necessitates regular monitoring, review, and revision of treatment approaches. Individuals with type 1 diabetes can effectively manage their illness and live a healthy, meaningful life if they take an informed and proactive attitude.

Type 1 Diabetes Lifestyle Changes

While type 1 diabetes is a life-altering diagnosis, it does not exclude a happy and healthy live. It does, however, need particular adaptations in daily living. Diet, exercise, stress management, and frequent health checks are the most important changes.

Dietary Guidelines

Diet is one of the most important lifestyle modifications. Type 1 diabetics should eat a well-balanced, healthful diet. This doesn't mean people have to give up all of their favorite foods or follow a strict diet of "diabetic foods." It's about eating a well-balanced diet that keeps blood glucose levels constant, offers necessary nutrients, and keeps them at a healthy weight. Carbohydrate counting, sometimes known as "carb counting," is a widespread strategy used by people with type 1 diabetes to regulate their blood glucose levels. Because carbs impact glucose levels more than any other nutrient, knowing how much carbohydrates are in a meal enables for correct insulin dosage changes. It gives persons with type 1 diabetes greater meal options while still regulating their blood glucose levels.

Exercising and Physical Activity

Physical exercise is an important part of controlling type 1 diabetes. Exercise provides various advantages, including improved insulin sensitivity, weight maintenance, and general cardiovascular health. The American Diabetes Association advises 150 minutes of moderate-intensity aerobic activity per week (such as brisk walking) and two to three sessions of resistance exercise per week. Physical exercise, on the other hand, can drop blood glucose levels, which may demand changes in insulin dosages or meal planning to avoid hypoglycemia (low blood sugar). Individuals with type 1 diabetes should work with their healthcare practitioner to develop an activity plan that meets their needs and is consistent with their overall diabetes management strategy.

Stress Reduction

Stress has a significant influence on blood glucose levels. Blood glucose levels can rise as a result of both physical stress (such as sickness or injury) and emotional stress (from personal or work-related concerns). As a result, stress management strategies are an essential component of the lifestyle adjustments required to control type 1 diabetes. Mindfulness and meditation, progressive muscle relaxation, deep breathing exercises, and other relaxation techniques are examples of techniques.

Health Checks on a Regular Basis

Routine health examinations are an important element of controlling type 1 diabetes. Regular medical visits are required to monitor the disease, make appropriate treatment plan modifications, and check for any diabetes-related complications, such as eye, kidney, or heart issues. It is also advised to get an annual flu vaccine as well as a pneumococcal disease vaccine. People with type 1 diabetes are more likely to have significant complications from certain infections, and these immunizations can help to lower that risk. In summary, type 1 diabetes management include making intelligent dietary choices, keeping a regular physical exercise routine, effectively managing stress, and attending frequent medical check-ups. The objective is to keep blood glucose levels as close to normal as possible while also preventing or managing the different problems that might occur with type 1 diabetes. Individuals with type 1 diabetes can live a healthy, active life by making certain lifestyle adjustments and adhering to a strict treatment regimen.

Chapter 3: Living With Type 2 Diabetes

An Overview of Type 2 Diabetes

Type 2 diabetes, also known as adult-onset diabetes or non-insulin-dependent diabetes, is a chronic disease that alters how the body metabolizes glucose (sugar). Type 2 diabetes has become more common in the United States and across the world in recent decades, along with rising obesity rates and sedentary lifestyles. The physiology of type 2 diabetes revolves mostly around insulin resistance. Insulin is a hormone generated by the pancreas's beta cells that helps cells in the body to absorb glucose and utilize it for energy. The cells of the body grow resistant to the effects of insulin in type 2 diabetes. In order to overcome this resistance, the pancreas generates more insulin. However, the pancreas may be unable to keep up with the growing demand over time, resulting in inadequate insulin production. Because glucose cannot enter the cells efficiently, this series of events causes an increase in blood glucose levels. Instead, it accumulates in the bloodstream, resulting in diabetic symptoms and consequences.

Type 2 diabetes symptoms frequently develop slowly over several years, and the illness can affect numerous sections of the body during this period. Increased thirst and urination, increased appetite, weight loss, weariness, hazy eyesight, slow-healing wounds, and recurrent infections are some of the symptoms. One important distinction between type 2 and type 1 diabetes is its substantial relationship with lifestyle variables. While type 1 diabetes is an autoimmune illness that cannot be avoided, a considerable number of type 2 diabetes cases may be averted with lifestyle changes. Obesity, physical inactivity, a poor diet, and advanced age all raise the chance of acquiring type 2 diabetes. It is crucial to remember, however, that not everyone with these risk factors develops the condition. This shows that genetics have a role in the disease's progression. According to research, those who have a family history of type 2 diabetes are more likely to get the disease, especially if the relative is a close family member like a parent or sibling. If type 2 diabetes is not adequately treated, it can lead to major problems such as cardiovascular disease, nerve damage (neuropathy), kidney damage (nephropathy), eye damage (retinopathy), and foot damage. Individuals with type 2 diabetes, however, can live productive, meaningful lives with proper care, which involves lifestyle changes and, in many cases, medicines. We will go deeper into the causes, risk factors, symptoms, diagnosis, and management of type 2 diabetes in the following parts, with the goal of providing a full understanding of the illness. Finally, while type 2 diabetes is a chronic disease, it is also treatable, and persons with this condition may take proactive actions to improve their health outcomes.

Type 2 Diabetes Management: Medication, Diet, and Exercise

Type 2 diabetes treatment is a comprehensive strategy that includes a combination of drugs, nutrition, and physical exercise, and it is largely targeted at regulating blood glucose levels to prevent the disease's long-term effects. Effective diabetes management necessitates collaboration between the patient and their healthcare practitioner, as well as the involvement of additional healthcare experts such as dietitians and diabetes educators. Metformin is the most often prescribed prescription for type 2 diabetes. It works by decreasing the quantity of glucose released into the bloodstream by the liver and increasing the sensitivity of the body's cells to insulin. If metformin alone is not enough, additional medication types such as sulfonylureas, thiazolidinediones, DPP-4 inhibitors, SGLT2 inhibitors, and GLP-1 receptor agonists may be supplemented or used instead. Insulin treatment may be required in some circumstances. The selection of medicine is extremely personal and is influenced by a variety of circumstances, including the patient's blood glucose levels, other health problems, and the medication's potential negative effects. Another important aspect of type 2 diabetes care is dietary adjustment. Maintaining a balanced diet can greatly assist persons with type 2 diabetes regulate their blood glucose levels and body weight. A dietician may assist in developing a meal plan that is tailored to the patient's health objectives, food choices, and lifestyle. A diabetes-friendly diet is high in whole grains, fruits and vegetables, lean proteins, and healthy fats, but low in processed foods, saturated and trans fats, and added sweets. Physical activity is also essential. Regular exercise helps keep blood glucose levels in a healthy range by controlling the quantity of glucose in the blood and increasing the body's sensitivity to insulin. Exercise also helps with weight control, heart health, stress reduction, and overall well-being. The American Diabetes Association advises at least 150 minutes of moderate-intensity aerobic physical activity per week or 75 minutes of vigorous-intensity aerobic physical activity per week, as well as muscle-strengthening exercises on two or more days each week. However, any physical exercise is preferable than none, and persons with diabetes should be encouraged to move more in their everyday lives. Self-monitoring of blood glucose levels is also an important part of management. Patients may make educated decisions about their day-to-day care with regular testing because they understand how diet, physical activity, medicine, and other variables impact their blood glucose levels. Another important part of treatment is patient education.

Diabetes patients should be taught on their disease, its complications, and how to manage it. They should be aware of the significance of frequent medical check-ups and screenings for potential issues, such as eye examinations, foot exams, and kidney function and cardiovascular health checks. To summarize, controlling type 2 diabetes requires a multifaceted, patient-centered strategy that includes medication, dietary changes, physical exercise, blood glucose self-monitoring, and patient education. People with type 2 diabetes can live a healthy, active life with proper care. However, it's important to realize that treatment tactics might vary widely from person to person, underlining the need of tailored care in diabetes control.

Type 2 Diabetes Lifestyle Changes

Successfully managing type 2 diabetes necessitates a number of significant lifestyle modifications. Although medicine is usually required, lifestyle adjustments can considerably increase the efficacy of medical therapy and, in rare situations, even help persons maintain normal blood glucose levels without medication. Adopting a balanced, healthy diet is one of the most beneficial lifestyle adjustments that a person with type 2 diabetes can undertake. This does not always imply strict diets or giving up all of one's favorite foods, but rather making more informed decisions about what and when to consume. It is advised that high-fiber meals, whole grains, fruits, vegetables, and lean meats be included, while saturated and trans fats, salt, and added sugars be avoided. Portion control is another important factor to remember, especially while eating nutritious foods. Spreading carbohydrate intake throughout the day can also help minimize blood glucose rises and keep energy levels stable. Physical activity is another important lifestyle improvement. Exercise not only helps with weight loss, but it also increases insulin sensitivity, allowing the body to use glucose more efficiently. Most days of the week, aim for at least 30 minutes of moderate-intensity activity, such as brisk walking, cycling, or swimming. Incorporating strength training activities twice a week might also be beneficial. Before beginning any fitness program, it is best to talk with a healthcare expert, especially if you have been inactive or have other health issues. Weight control is essential in the treatment of type 2 diabetes. Insulin resistance has been related to excess body weight, particularly around the waist. As a result, even a small amount of weight loss can enhance insulin sensitivity and glycemic management.

A healthy weight may be attained and maintained by combining a balanced diet with frequent physical exercise. Quitting smoking is critical. It has been demonstrated that smoking raises blood glucose levels and causes insulin resistance. It also raises the risk of diabetic complications such as heart disease, renal disease, and nerve damage. Individuals who smoke should be encouraged and supported in their efforts to stop. It is also recommended that you limit your alcohol consumption. Depending on the amount drank and whether it is drunk with food, alcohol can induce either high or low blood glucose levels. If diabetics want to drink, they should do it in moderation and never on an empty stomach. It is critical to check blood glucose levels on a regular basis. It contains useful information on how certain diets, activities, and other variables impact blood glucose levels. This information may be used to make medication, diet planning, and physical activity decisions. Finally, routine check-ups and screens for problems are essential. Eye exams, foot checks, blood pressure measurements, lipid profile testing, and kidney function tests are all part of the package. Finally, controlling type 2 diabetes necessitates a multifaceted strategy that includes not just medical therapy but also extensive lifestyle modifications. It is crucial to emphasize that these adjustments are intended to promote general health and well-being as well as diabetes management. It's a long-term commitment, but the rewards are great, both in terms of controlling the disease and improving quality of life.

Chapter 4: Living With Gestational Diabetes

Knowledge of Gestational Diabetes

A kind of diabetes known as gestational diabetes mellitus (GDM) affects pregnant women and often goes away after the baby is delivered. Despite being transient, gestational diabetes is a serious illness that needs to be carefully managed to protect both the mother and the unborn child's health and wellbeing. Gestational diabetes is thought to affect 2% to 10% of pregnancies annually in the United States. Although the illness can develop at any point in pregnancy, it is often identified in the second or third trimester. Pregnancy-related diabetes, like other types, affects how the body's cells use glucose, a type of sugar that serves as our body's main fuel source. The placenta, which links the fetus to the mother's blood supply, secretes high quantities of many additional hormones throughout pregnancy. Nearly all of them cause insulin to work less effectively in the cells, which results in insulin resistance. The placenta generates more of these hormones as the baby develops, which increases insulin resistance.

Gestational diabetes essentially develops when the pancreas is unable to generate enough insulin to counteract the impact of the hormones released during pregnancy. High blood sugar levels result from the inability of glucose to be properly converted into energy, which causes it to accumulate in the bloodstream. Because the illness frequently has mild symptoms, screening for it is an essential component of prenatal treatment. If left untreated, it may harm the unborn child's development and the pregnancy. Pre-eclampsia, a dangerous pregnancy condition defined by elevated blood pressure, is more likely to affect mothers with gestational diabetes.

They are also more likely to have large-for-gestational-age babies, which can complicate labor and increase the chance of a cesarean surgery. Babies whose moms have gestational diabetes are at risk for a number of health issues. Jaundice, hypoglycemia, and respiratory distress syndrome, a disorder that makes breathing challenging, are a few of them. Later in adulthood, they may also have an increased chance of developing type 2 diabetes and obesity. Additionally, having gestational diabetes raises a woman's likelihood of later getting type 2 diabetes. Maintaining a healthy lifestyle after giving birth becomes crucial for these people. Following childbirth, routine blood glucose monitoring can help with the early diagnosis and management of type 2 diabetes. According to risk factors, women who are overweight, have polycystic ovarian syndrome, have had gestational diabetes in a prior pregnancy, have a family history of diabetes, or who are overweight are more likely to develop gestational diabetes.

African Americans, Hispanic/Latino Americans, American Indians, people from the Pacific Islands, and certain Asian Americans are among the racial and ethnic groups who are more at risk. In conclusion, gestational diabetes is a serious illness that has to be carefully monitored and managed. Gestational diabetes can be successfully managed by good screening and treatment techniques, protecting both the mother and the unborn child's health. The first step in this procedure is to comprehend the subtleties of the illness.

Gestational Diabetes Management

The major goal of gestational diabetes management is to keep pregnant women's blood sugar levels normal. This objective necessitates a multifaceted strategy that includes frequent blood glucose testing, dietary adjustments, exercise, and, in some circumstances, the use of medication. The initial step in controlling gestational diabetes is routine blood glucose monitoring. If the disease is detected in a pregnant woman, she may need to test her blood sugar several times a day, frequently before and after meals. Understanding how nutrition, activity, and medicine impact blood glucose levels is much easier with the use of this monitoring. It is the cornerstone of gestational diabetes management since it offers crucial information needed to change diet or medication as needed. The cornerstone of controlling gestational diabetes is dietary change. A licensed dietician can assist in creating a diet that guarantees the mother and child get the nutrients they need without raising their blood sugar levels. Proteins, carbs, and fats are normally balanced in the diet, and frequent meals and snacks are encouraged to prevent blood sugar swings. In general, the diet plan prioritizes complete foods like fruits, vegetables, lean meats, and whole grains while limiting processed meals that are heavy in sugar and bad fats. Another critical component of treating gestational diabetes is consistent physical exercise. Exercise encourages the body's cells to take up glucose for energy, lowering the amount of glucose in the circulation and lowering blood sugar levels. Swimming, prenatal fitness courses, and brisk walking are all safe kinds of exercise during pregnancy.

Before beginning an exercise program, however, women with gestational diabetes must discuss it with their healthcare practitioner since some may need to modify their activity levels in light of their medical history and the particulars of their pregnancy. Occasionally, dietary adjustments and increased physical activity may not be sufficient to keep blood glucose levels within the desired range. In such cases, medication can be required. The most typical drug used to treat gestational diabetes is insulin. By instructing cells to absorb glucose from the circulation, it aids in controlling the body's glucose levels. Oral drugs like metformin or glyburide can also be utilized, however a healthcare practitioner should always be consulted before selecting a medication and administering it. Another crucial part of controlling gestational diabetes is keeping an eye out for any complications. Prenatal checkups on a regular basis enable early diagnosis of any issues, such as high blood pressure or early labor symptoms. Given that women who have experienced prenatal diabetes are more likely to subsequently acquire type 2 diabetes, postpartum care, including blood glucose monitoring, is particularly essential.

Last but not least, providing emotional support is crucial in treating gestational diabetes. A person's general health and blood glucose levels might be affected by psychological stress. Therefore, it may be advantageous to ask for help from family, friends, support groups, or mental health specialists. Final thoughts: Regular blood glucose testing, dietary and lifestyle changes, and maybe medication use are all part of controlling gestational diabetes. It is totally feasible for women with gestational diabetes to experience a successful pregnancy and delivery while lowering their risk of developing diabetes later in life. It emphasizes the need of a personalized treatment plan and continual contact with the medical staff.

Post-Pregnancy Considerations

The worry for the mother's and child's health does not end if gestational diabetes is adequately managed throughout pregnancy. To guarantee that the mother's blood glucose levels return to normal and that both the mother and child are healthy throughout the post-pregnancy period, careful monitoring and targeted treatment are necessary. During this time, there may be a window of opportunity for preventative healthcare actions to reduce future health risks for both the mother and the child. After birth, blood sugar levels in the majority of women quickly recover to normal. Testing must be done in order to verify this, though. Six to twelve weeks after giving birth, the American Diabetes Association advises women with a history of gestational diabetes to have a 75-gram oral glucose tolerance test.

This test determines if the lady has become prediabetic or has developed type 2 diabetes, or whether she has returned to a non-diabetic condition. Type 2 diabetes is far more likely to strike women who have experienced gestational diabetes later in life. Nearly half of all women with gestational diabetes are predicted to acquire type 2 diabetes within ten years of giving birth. Therefore, it is highly advised to maintain lifelong surveillance for the emergence of diabetes or prediabetes. A balanced diet, frequent exercise, and occasional blood glucose testing are all part of a healthy lifestyle. Ideally, this occurs once a year. The importance of breastfeeding as a component of post-partum care for moms with gestational diabetes warrants special consideration.

It offers a number of advantages, including assisting the mother in losing pregnancy weight and using extra glucose in the body to reduce blood sugar levels. Furthermore, studies have indicated that breastfeeding lowers the baby's chance of growing up overweight and getting type 2 diabetes. A mother with gestational diabetes who gives birth has to be closely watched as well. These kids have a higher chance of being obese and getting type 2 diabetes later in life. Pediatricians will keep an eye on the child's development, weight, and general health, and parents will receive recommendations on how to foster a good diet and active lifestyle from an early age. There are repercussions for future pregnancies from a previous incident of gestational diabetes. Women who have had gestational diabetes are more likely to do so in future pregnancies.

As a result, before trying to get pregnant again, pre-pregnancy counseling should be provided to go over the significance of reaching a healthy weight and improving glycemic control. Before the subsequent pregnancy and early in the first trimester, blood glucose levels should be monitored to make sure they are within a normal range. It's crucial to keep in mind that while gestational diabetes raises the chance of specific health problems, it does not ensure they will materialize. Women may considerably lower their risk and living long lives by changing to a healthy lifestyle and getting frequent checkups. Instead of being seen with fear, the post-pregnancy era following gestational diabetes should be seen as a chance to improve both the mother's and the child's lifestyle.

Chapter 5: Nutrition and Diabetes

The Role of Diet in Diabetes Management

Diabetes control relies heavily on nutrition. In addition to having a direct impact on blood sugar levels, it also has an impact on other risk factors including body weight, blood pressure, and cholesterol levels. In order to properly regulate these variables and treat diabetes holistically, a well-balanced diet is essential. The major objectives of nutritional management in diabetes are cholesterol and blood pressure control, as well as achieving and maintaining appropriate blood glucose levels. Consuming a diet high in whole grains, fruits, vegetables, lean proteins, and healthy fats while minimizing intake of saturated fats, sweets, and salt is the best way to achieve this aim. A balanced diet is necessary for managing diabetes and includes not only what to eat but also when to eat and how much to consume. Blood glucose levels are most significantly influenced by carbohydrates. It's not about removing them from the diet; it's about knowing how to choose and balance the proper carbs.

Complex carbs, such as those found in whole grains, fruits, vegetables, and legumes, are healthier for people with diabetes because they raise blood glucose levels more gradually than refined carbohydrates do. Dietary fiber is a further essential dietary component for controlling diabetes. Fiber reduces the pace at which carbs are digested and absorbed, causing blood glucose levels to rise more gradually. A high-fiber diet can lower the risk of cardiovascular disease, a major consequence of diabetes, and help regulate blood glucose levels. Protein is an essential component of a diabetic diet since it can help regulate appetite and has no effect on blood glucose levels. Lean proteins must be chosen, nevertheless, in order to reduce your intake of saturated fat. Excellent sources of lean protein include fish, skinless poultry, lean meats, eggs, low-fat dairy, lentils, and soy products.

Additionally, fats—particularly heart-healthy unsaturated fats—play a significant role. Although they don't directly alter blood sugar levels, they can have an impact on insulin resistance and cardiovascular health. Healthy fats may be found in foods like avocados, olives, nuts, seeds, and seafood like mackerel and salmon. Both timing and quantity control are essential for controlling blood sugar levels. To avoid blood sugar peaks and falls, it's important to consume regular meals and snacks. A healthy weight and avoiding overeating are two further benefits of paying attention to portion sizes, both of which are essential for treating diabetes. The type and stage of diabetes, as well as age, gender, exercise level, and current health state, can all affect an individual's dietary requirements. Consequently, receiving tailored dietary guidance from a qualified dietitian or a certified diabetes educator can be very helpful.

These experts can assist people with diabetes in developing a meal plan that suits their unique health objectives, dietary choices, and lifestyle. In conclusion, maintaining a healthy diet is essential for controlling diabetes. By assisting in the management of body weight and cardiovascular health, it has a direct impact on blood glucose control and a secondary effect on overall health. The ultimate goal should be to incorporate food management into a thorough diabetic treatment plan that also includes medication (if necessary), physical exercise, and routine health examinations. It is more important to develop a sustainable way of life than to follow a limited "diabetic diet."

Understanding Carbohydrates, Proteins, and Fats

Understanding the three main nutrients—carbohydrates, proteins, and fats—and how they affect the body's metabolism, particularly in persons with diabetes, is the first step in understanding how food affects diabetes treatment.

Carbohydrates

The body uses carbohydrates as its main fuel source. They are digested and converted to glucose, which enters the circulation and raises blood glucose levels. However, not all carbs have the same effects on blood sugar levels. Based on their chemical makeup, carbohydrates can be divided into simple and complicated categories. Simple carbohydrates, such as those found in sugar, soda, and syrup, have a more easily digestible molecular structure that makes them more likely to cause an increase in blood sugar levels. The breakdown of complex carbs, such as those found in whole grains, fruits, and vegetables, takes longer and results in a slower increase in blood glucose levels.

Proteins

Proteins are necessary for hormone production, immune system health, and cell development and repair. Unlike carbs, when ingested in moderation, proteins have very little impact on blood glucose levels. High protein intake, particularly from animal sources, can, however, raise cholesterol and harmful saturated fat intake, raising the risk of heart disease. Lean proteins and plant-based proteins are advised as a result.

Fats

Like carbs and proteins, fats are an essential component of the diet because they are essential for many physiological processes, such as hormone generation and nutrient absorption. However, the kind of fat is very important. Avocados, nuts, seeds, and fatty fish are examples of foods high in unsaturated fats that can help improve heart health by lowering "bad" LDL cholesterol levels and raising "good" HDL cholesterol. On the other side, saturated fats, which may be found in meals like red meat and full-fat dairy products, can raise LDL cholesterol levels, which increases the risk of heart disease. Consuming a diet that balances these three crucial nutrients will help regulate blood sugar levels and improve general health when it comes to diabetes.

For a person with diabetes, a balanced diet may resemble this:

- **Carbo**: 45–60% of daily calories should come from carbs, with a focus on complex carbohydrates and foods high in fiber to control blood sugar levels after meals.
- **Protein**: Lean proteins and sources from plants are preferred to increase consumption of unsaturated fats in the protein category, which accounts for 15–20% of daily calories.
- **Fat**: 20–35% of total daily calories should come from fats, with trans and saturated fat intake being kept to a minimum to protect heart health.

Last but not least, it's critical to keep in mind that every person's body reacts differently to various meals and diets. To understand how various foods impact your blood glucose levels, it is essential to monitor blood glucose levels both before and after meals. A registered dietitian or a certified diabetes educator can offer individualized guidance based on dietary requirements and health objectives. Keep in mind that regulating blood glucose levels is just one aspect of maintaining overall health. Adopting a balanced and varied diet, together with regular exercise and medication (if required), can improve a person with diabetes's overall health and quality of life.

What Is the Glycemic Index and Why Does It Matter?

The Glycemic Index (GI), which gives people a detailed understanding of how various carbohydrate-containing diets impact blood glucose levels, is a helpful tool in the treatment of diabetes. The GI compares a food to a reference food, generally pure glucose or white bread, to determine how much of an effect the food has on the rise in blood glucose levels two hours after intake. A score is assigned to each dish on a range of 0 to 100, with higher numbers denoting a bigger rise in blood sugar levels. Diabetes management may be significantly impacted by comprehending and using the GI. It can serve as a nutritional roadmap, assisting people in choosing foods that cause blood glucose levels to increase more gradually and gradually. In regulating post-meal or "postprandial" blood glucose levels, a crucial component of total blood glucose control, this is very helpful. Foods with a high GI (70 or higher on the GI scale) are digested and absorbed quickly, causing blood glucose levels to rise sharply and quickly. White bread, the majority of white rices, corn flakes, and meals high in glucose are other examples. In contrast, meals with a low GI (55 or less on the GI scale) take longer to digest and absorb, which causes blood sugar levels to gradually rise. These consist of non-starchy vegetables, whole grains, fruits like apples and oranges, and legumes. Foods with a moderate glycemic index (GI) range from 56 to 69 result in a modest increase in blood sugar levels. This group includes foods like whole grains, brown rice, sweet potatoes, and some fruits like grapes and bananas. The GI, however, is not a stand-alone manual for a healthy diet.

The GI of a meal does not reveal any details about its nutritional makeup. While certain high-GI meals may be low in calories and high in vital nutrients, other low-GI foods may be heavy in calories, fat, or salt. The Glycemic Load (GL), which takes into consideration the quantity of carbohydrates in a portion of food as well as how rapidly it rises blood sugar levels, is another aspect to take into account. It may provide a clearer picture of how a food affects blood sugar levels. Furthermore, a number of elements, such as a food's ripeness, preparation method, and accompanying ingredients, might affect its GI. The GI of the same food might vary depending on whether it is eaten alone or as a meal. A meal's total GI can be reduced by include high-GI meals with protein, fat, or fiber. As a result, even though the Glycemic Index can be a helpful tool for managing post-meal blood glucose levels in people with diabetes, it should be used in conjunction with other variables such as total carbohydrate intake, food nutritional value, the Glycemic Load, and individual blood glucose responses.

A certified dietitian or a healthcare provider can offer individualized guidance on how to combine the GI's principles into a balanced, healthy eating plan. Although diet is only one component of managing diabetes, with the correct information and tools, it may be an effective tool for preserving blood glucose control and enhancing general health. Making a Balanced Meal Plan, Section

Creating a Balanced Meal Plan

In order to effectively manage diabetes, a balanced food plan must be made. Not only must the sort of food be taken into account, but also its time and amount. A balanced diet seeks to maintain steady blood sugar levels, avoid sharp ups and downs, supply necessary nutrients, and keep the body at a healthy weight. The macronutrients carbs, proteins, and fats must be balanced in a diabetic diet plan. To ensure that the body gets all the vitamins and minerals it needs, it's crucial to eat a variety of meals. Approximately 50% of the calories might come from carbs, 20% from protein, and the remaining 30% from healthy fats. The majority of your daily intake of carbohydrates need to come from complex foods with a low Glycemic Index (GI), such whole grains, legumes, fruits, and non-starchy vegetables. The blood glucose levels rise gradually as a result of these meals' sluggish digestion.

The American Diabetes Association advises consuming at least 14 grams of fiber for every 1,000 calories ingested because fiber reduces blood sugar increases by reducing the rate at which sugar enters the system. Lean sources of protein should be consumed, such as fish, poultry, eggs, lentils, and low-fat dairy foods. Protein does not significantly affect blood glucose levels and is necessary for the development and repair of bodily tissues. Prioritize monounsaturated and polyunsaturated fats, which may be found in foods like avocados, olives, almonds, seeds, and fatty seafood like salmon. These lipids have the ability to raise levels of "good" HDL cholesterol while decreasing "bad" LDL cholesterol levels. Here is an example of a seven-day diabetic eating plan.

Approximately 1600–1800 calories per day are provided by this diet, of which 45–50% are from carbs, 20–20% from protein, and 35–35% from fats:

Day 1

- For breakfast, have some steel-cut oats, blueberries, and almonds.
- For lunch, a salad of grilled chicken, mixed greens, tomatoes, cucumbers, olives, and vinaigrette dressing.
- Quinoa and steamed broccoli with baked salmon for dinner.
- Snacks: a tiny apple and some hummus-topped carrot sticks

Day 2

- Eggs scrambled with spinach and whole grain bread for breakfast
- Lunch: a side salad and lentil soup Dinner will be grilled shrimp over brown rice and a variety of veggies.
- Snacks: A single orange and few walnuts

Day 3

- For breakfast, combine Greek yogurt with a variety of berries and chia seeds.
- A turkey sandwich on whole-wheat bread with lettuce, tomato, and avocado for lunch
- Grilled chicken breast, sweet potato, and green beans for dinner
- Snacks: a tiny pear and a stick of string cheese with less fat

This is only an illustration, and individual needs may change depending on things like age, sex, weight, amount of physical activity, and certain dietary preferences or constraints. Based on distinct requirements and interests, a licensed dietitian can offer individualized guidance on meal planning. Last but not least, keep in mind that treating diabetes entails more than simply nutrition. A complete diabetes treatment strategy includes regular physical exercise, taking prescribed medications, monitoring blood glucose levels, and frequent check-ups with your healthcare professional.

Chapter 6: Food Guide for Diabetes

Food to eat

It's crucial to pay attention to what you eat if you have diabetes and are controlling it. Our decisions can have a big effect on how well we feel, how well our blood sugar levels are doing. In order to maintain stable blood sugar levels and support optimum health, it's crucial to concentrate on nutrient-dense diets. Dietary fiber-rich diets are one group of foods that are advantageous for diabetics. Sugars are absorbed more gradually by fiber, reducing the likelihood of blood sugar rises. A great source of dietary fiber is whole grains. Brown rice, oatmeal, quinoa, and whole grain bread and pasta are a few examples of them. Look for items that claim "whole grain" as the first component when selecting bread or pasta. Similar to how they are high in fiber, fruits and vegetables should account for a large portion of a diabetic diet. They are also loaded with antioxidants, vitamins, and minerals that support general health. But it's important to take the glycemic index of fruits into account and eat them in moderation. With a lower glycemic index, berries, cherries, peaches, apricots, apples, oranges, and pears are all excellent options. Another crucial element of a diabetic-friendly diet is lean proteins. Lean protein may be found in abundance in foods like skinless chicken, turkey, fish, eggs, tofu, and low-fat dairy products.

These foods can support feelings of fullness and have negligible to no impact on blood glucose levels. A balanced food plan should also contain healthy fats. Monounsaturated and polyunsaturated fats are abundant in avocados, olives, nuts, seeds, and fatty fish like salmon and mackerel. These lipids have the ability to raise levels of "good" HDL cholesterol while decreasing "bad" LDL cholesterol levels. They also supply the body with vital fatty acids, which it cannot make on its own. Vegetables without starch are essential to a diabetic diet. Leafy greens, broccoli, bell peppers, zucchini, tomatoes, cucumber, and many more foods fall under this category. Non-starchy veggies are great for balancing blood sugar levels since they are low in carbohydrates and high in fiber. Last but not least, legumes like lentils, chickpeas, and different kinds of beans are quite advantageous. They are a great option for preserving stable blood sugar levels since they are a rich source of protein and fiber. Naturally, it's important to keep in mind that every individual is unique and that what works for one person might not work for another. A number of variables, such as the type of diabetes, lifestyle, tastes, and more, might affect the ideal nutritional strategy for treating diabetes. It is advised to work closely with a medical professional or a qualified dietitian to create a customized meal plan that meets certain dietary requirements and preferences. In conclusion, people with diabetes can benefit greatly from a balanced, nutrient-dense diet that is rich in fiber, lean proteins, healthy fats, and low-glycemic fruits and vegetables. This will help to control blood sugar levels and will also help to promote general health. A balanced diet can help with optimal diabetes treatment, along with regular exercise and medication (if recommended).

Following is a list of foods to eat:

Complete Grains:

- Brown Rice
- Oatmeal
- Quinoa
- Whole-wheat bread
- Whole-wheat pasta

Glycemic index-lower fruits:

- Berries
- Cherries
- Peaches
- Apricots

- Apples
- Oranges
- Pears

Healthy proteins:

- Chicken without skin
- Turkey
- Fish
- Eggs
- Tofu
- Dairy products with low fat

Suitable Fats:

- Avocados
- Olives
- Nuts
- Seeds
- Fatty fish, such as mackerel and salmon

Vegetables without a starch:

- Greens with leaves

- Broccoli
- Peppers
- Zucchini
- Tomatoes
- Cucumbers

Legumes:

- Lentils
- Chickpeas
- Beans

Foods to Avoid

Knowing what to avoid is just as important for managing diabetes as what to eat. An unhealthy food-rich diet can worsen diabetes symptoms, raise the risk of complications, and result in uncontrolled blood glucose levels. Drinks with added sugar: Sports drinks, sweet tea, soda, and fruit juice all contain a staggering amount of carbs. They may result in abrupt blood sugar rises, which may make it harder to manage diabetes. Additionally, these beverages frequently have a lot of calories and little nutritious benefit. Unsaturated fatty acids are made more stable by the addition of hydrogen to produce trans fats. Many processed foods, including crackers, baked products, and even certain margarines, contain trans fats. They should be avoided as much as possible because they are well known for having detrimental impacts on heart health. White bread, pasta, and rice are created from refined grains, meaning that the bran and germ have been removed during processing. In addition to removing fiber and minerals, this technique produces foods with a high glycemic index.

These are not recommended for those with diabetes since eating them might cause significant blood sugar rises. Fruit-flavored yogurt is frequently loaded with sugar, despite the fact that it can be a nutritious meal option. Instead, use plain yogurt and flavor it with fresh fruit. Breakfast cereals with added sugar: Breakfast cereals, particularly those targeted toward youngsters, can include a lot of sugar. Always check the nutritional information and choose low-sugar, high-fiber foods. Coffee drinks with flavors: Pure coffee doesn't cause blood sugar levels to rise. However, flavored coffee beverages frequently include a lot of sugar and can raise blood sugar levels. The better option is a standard cup of coffee or an espresso with a little milk or cream. Although they are all-natural sweeteners, honey, agave nectar, and maple syrup include a lot of carbs and can raise blood sugar levels. Fried Foods: Foods rich in harmful fats and carbs include fried snacks, french fries, and fried poultry.

They may cause weight gain and make it more difficult to control diabetes. Alcohol: Alcohol can affect how well diabetic treatments work and the blood sugar levels in the body. If you do decide to drink, make sure to do it occasionally and with meals. It is important to remember that each person is different and that everyone's reactions to food might vary. In order to understand how various meals influence your personal health, it's critical to check your blood sugar levels and consult with a healthcare provider, even though this list just serves as a basic reference. You may effectively control diabetic symptoms and lower the risk of complications by actively regulating your diet.

Sweet Drinks

- Common soda
- Fruit soda
- Energy beverages
- Sweet chai
- Other sweet beverages

Foods High in Trans Fat

- Baked items from the store (cookies, cakes)
- Quick meals (burgers, fries)
- Prepackaged snacks (cookies, chips)
- Frozen meals

- Flavored syrup-infused lattes

Refined Grains

- bread
- White noodles
- Plain rice
- Bagels

Sweeteners

- Honey Nectar from agave
- Maple sugar

Sweetened Dairy Products

- Yogurt with flavors
- Sugared milk
- Dessert Added Sugar to Breakfast Foods
- Sweet cereals
- Syrup-topped pancakes
- Customary jellies and jams

Fried Meals

- Chicken fingers
- Potato chips
- Doughnuts
- The onion ring

Sugary coffee beverages

- Frappuccino
- Mochas

Alcoholic Drinks

- Beer
- Sugary wines
- Liqueurs

Reading and Understanding Food Labels

Understanding how to read and comprehend food labels is a crucial skill for people with diabetes since it has a significant impact on their health outcomes. Due to the avalanche of numbers, percentages, and scientific jargon on nutrition labels, it may often be difficult to understand the information they provide regarding a food item's nutritional composition. This section tries to clarify how to successfully read food labels and apply this information in the context of managing diabetes. The serving size is the first thing to look at on a food label. It's important to keep in mind that all nutritional data is per serving, not necessarily per package. For instance, if a serving size of 15 chips is specified on a bag of potato chips, and you eat the entire bag—which has eight servings—you would consume eight times the amount of calories, carbs, and other nutrients that are shown in each serving. The amount of calories in each serving should be considered after deciding the serving size. The amount of energy you get from a serving of this meal is measured in calories. Calorie counting is essential, especially if losing weight is a goal of your diabetes control strategy. The breakdown of nutrients follows, which include details on total fat, cholesterol, salt, total carbs, and protein. Since they have the most noticeable immediate impact on blood sugar levels, carbs are usually your main area of attention if you're controlling diabetes. It's crucial to take into account the different kinds of carbs present, though. Find foods that are low in sugars, especially added sugars, and high in dietary fiber.

While additional sweets can boost blood sugar and contribute to weight gain, dietary fiber can help control blood sugar levels and maintain a healthy weight. Beyond carbs, patients with diabetes should also take salt, cholesterol, and saturated and trans fats into account because these nutrients might increase blood pressure and heart disease risk. In general, it is best to avoid or consume these foods in moderation. Vitamins and minerals will also be listed on the food label. Despite the fact that they have no direct impact on blood sugar levels, they are crucial for general health. As a result, those who have diabetes should focus on eating meals high in vital minerals including potassium, calcium, iron, and vitamins A and C. The list of components might also offer important information. Ingredients are ordered from top to lowest in terms of the quantity they make up the dish. This list might aid in identifying harmful fats, added sugars, and other components that should be avoided. In conclusion, food labels are an essential tool for people with diabetes.

They offer vital details that can support making knowledgeable food selections, assisting with blood sugar regulation, weight management, and general health promotion. Therefore, knowing how to read and comprehend these labels is a crucial skill for managing diabetes successfully.

Chapter 7: Superfoods and Supplements

<u>Understanding Superfoods</u>

In the health and wellness sector, "superfood" has gained popularity. Superfoods are essentially foods that are thought to be very beneficial for one's health and wellbeing. They are nutrient-rich and provide a number of health advantages, including as lowering the chance of developing chronic illnesses like diabetes and heart disease. But it's important to comprehend what superfoods are and how they fit into a holistic diabetes management plan. Superfoods are often unprocessed or hardly processed foods that are rich in antioxidants, phytonutrients, fiber, vitamins, and minerals. These substances support excellent health, promote illness prevention, and improve both physical and mental function.

A balanced, nutritious diet can provide more health advantages than any one item, especially those dubbed "superfoods," it is crucial to remember this. Certain superfoods may have qualities that are especially advantageous in the setting of diabetes. Since they have a low glycemic index, many superfoods, for example, are less likely to trigger a sharp increase in blood sugar levels. Some superfoods are also anti-inflammatory, which is advantageous because chronic inflammation has been linked to insulin resistance, a major risk factor for type 2 diabetes.

Here are a few superfoods that are especially advantageous for people with diabetes:
- **Berries**: Berries are an abundant source of antioxidants, such as anthocyanins, which have been connected to improved insulin sensitivity and a lower risk of cancer and heart disease. They also have a low glycemic index and a lot of fiber.
- **Leafy Greens**: Due to their low calorie and carbohydrate content, leafy greens like spinach and kale can help control blood sugar levels. They include many of vitamins and minerals and are also strong in fiber.

- **Fish**: Omega-3 fatty acids, which are abundant in fatty fish like salmon, mackerel, sardines, and trout, have been found to decrease inflammation and cut the risk of heart disease, a major consequence of diabetes. Nuts and seeds are rich sources of dietary fiber and heart-healthy lipids. They can lower the risk of heart disease and aid in blood sugar regulation.
- **Whole Grains**: Whole grains have a lot of fiber, which helps reduce the absorption of sugar into your system and avoid increases in glucose levels.

Examples of whole grains include brown rice, oats, whole-grain bread, and pasta. Understanding superfoods and include them in your diet are important steps toward properly controlling diabetes. However, it's crucial to keep in mind that eating superfoods is not a replacement for a healthy diet or prescription drugs. They are a supplement to a whole strategy for treating diabetes, which also involves regular exercise, a balanced diet, frequent checkups, and taking prescription medicine as instructed by a healthcare provider.

Supplements for Diabetes Management

Dietary supplements are frequently thought of as supplementary therapy choices in the management of diabetes, but they should never take the place of a balanced diet, regular exercise, and prescription medicines. However, they can support these main methods by assisting in blood sugar regulation, enhancing insulin sensitivity, easing symptoms, and avoiding problems. This chapter focuses on the dietary supplements that are most frequently used to control diabetes and the research that backs them up. Chromium is one of the supplements for diabetic management that has been the subject of the most research. The metabolism of carbohydrates and fats is influenced by the trace element chromium. It's thought to strengthen how insulin works, which might improve blood sugar regulation.

Studies have shown mixed findings; some have suggested a slight influence on glycemic management, while others have found no appreciable difference. Although it is generally regarded as safe, it is always advised to talk with a healthcare professional before beginning any supplement program. Another mineral that has been researched in relation to diabetes is magnesium.

Magnesium is essential for the metabolism of insulin, and insulin resistance has been associated with magnesium shortage. Numerous studies indicate that taking supplemental magnesium may help diabetics with insulin sensitivity and blood sugar control, but further study is required.

An antioxidant called **alpha-lipoic acid** has been studied for its possible impact on diabetic neuropathy and insulin resistance. It may improve insulin sensitivity and reduce the course of nerve damage in diabetics, especially those with diabetic peripheral neuropathy, according to studies. To ascertain the ideal dose and long-term safety of this product, additional study is necessary.

Cinnamon is another dietary item that has been investigated for its possible advantages in treating diabetes. According to some research, cinnamon may increase insulin sensitivity while lowering blood sugar levels. However, further high-quality studies are required as prior study has not discovered any impact.

Last but not least, **fish oil** supplements are frequently used to augment omega-3 fatty acids, which are predominantly found in fatty fish. While omega-3s are well known for their heart health advantages, it is less understood how they affect blood glucose regulation. According to some study, they might aid diabetics in reducing their triglycerides—a kind of fat related to heart disease.

here are a number of key considerations when looking at supplements for managing diabetes. First, dietary supplements can have negative effects and interact negatively with drugs, particularly those used to treat diabetes. As a result, it's crucial to talk about any new supplement regimen with a healthcare professional, especially one who is knowledgeable with your medical history and the pharmacology of your prescription drugs. Second, because the Food and Drug Administration (FDA) does not monitor nutritional supplements as thoroughly as it does prescription pharmaceuticals, their quality and purity might vary. It's crucial to pick items from reliable producers that willingly submit them to third-party lab testing for quality assurance. Finally, while some supplements could be advantageous for those who have diabetes, they cannot take the place of an all-inclusive diabetes care strategy. They should be seen as possible instruments to support rather than replace established methods, such as a balanced diet, regular exercise, yearly physical exams, and prescription medicine.

Considerations and Precautions

It is crucial to remember a number of key factors before starting the route of supplement use for diabetes control. These safety measures are designed to protect the well-being of persons who choose to utilize supplements as a part of their diabetes treatment plan. The interactions between supplements and drugs should be taken into account initially. Numerous dietary supplements and over-the-counter and prescription medications may interact. These interactions may reduce a drug's efficacy, aggravate side effects, or result in other negative outcomes. For instance, chromium supplements may increase the effects of insulin and other glucose-lowering drugs, which, if not well regulated, might result in low blood sugar levels (hypoglycemia). Supplements with blood-thinning qualities, such fish oil, however, may interfere with anticoagulant drugs. It is crucial to let healthcare professionals know about all supplements used in order for them to check for any potential interactions with any prescription drugs.

The variation in supplement quality and purity is the second factor to take into account. Dietary supplements are not subject to the same tight rules as prescription drugs, which must adhere to the FDA's exacting quality control criteria. As a result, the quality, purity, and efficacy of supplements may vary significantly. It's possible for certain goods to have components that aren't indicated on the label or to lack the specified level of an active ingredient. As a result, it's essential to get supplements from reliable producers recognized for their strict quality control procedures. The potential negative effects of supplements are the third factor to take into account. Despite the fact that nutritional supplements are frequently thought of as natural and hence secure, this isn't always the case. Particularly when used in high dosages or in conjunction with other vitamins or drugs, some supplements might have negative effects. For instance, large dosages of magnesium might result in diarrhea, and consuming too much fish oil can have unfavorable side effects including nausea, diarrhea, and fishy breath. Before beginning any new supplement regimen, it's crucial to talk with a healthcare professional about any possible adverse effects. The significance of changing one's lifestyle is yet another important factor.

Although certain supplements may aid in the management of diabetes, they cannot replace a healthy lifestyle. The cornerstones of diabetes treatment continue to be a balanced diet, frequent physical exercise, keeping a healthy weight, routine blood glucose monitoring, and adherence to prescribed medicines. Supplements should be seen as complements to these lifestyle changes rather than as a replacement. Finally, remember that different people may react differently to supplements. One person's solution might not be suitable for another. How a person reacts to a certain supplement can be influenced by a variety of variables, including genetics, nutrition, lifestyle, and the type and severity of diabetes. While using supplements, it's crucial to frequently check blood sugar levels to assess their efficacy and, with a doctor's approval, modify dosages as needed. Given the wide variety of products on the market and the occasionally contradictory information on their efficacy, navigating the world of dietary supplements may be difficult. However, they have the potential to be effective weapons in the struggle against this chronic illness if the proper precautions are taken and their place within the larger context of diabetes care is understood.

Always consult a healthcare practitioner before beginning a new supplement regimen, and keep in mind that supplements should support rather than replace standard diabetic therapy.

Chapter 8: Mindful Eating

Understanding Mindful Eating

Mindful eating is a powerful tool that goes beyond what you eat, reaching into when, why, and how you eat. It introduces the concept of awareness into the often-mechanical act of consuming food. By tuning into the sensations of eating, the feelings that lead us to eat, and the effects of food on our bodies, we can transform our relationship with food and make wiser, healthier decisions. Mindful eating starts with recognition of hunger cues. This means paying attention to the physical signals your body sends when it needs nourishment. Hunger pangs, lack of energy, and rumbling in the stomach are all indications that your body is ready for food. By responding to these signals instead of eating according to a preset schedule, we can align our eating habits with our body's actual needs.

On the other hand, mindful eating also involves recognizing satiety cues or the signs that we have had enough to eat. Feeling comfortably full, a decrease in the taste of food, and a general loss of interest in eating further are all signs that we should stop eating. Ignoring these signals can lead to overeating, contributing to weight gain and increasing the risk of type 2 diabetes. Mindful eating encourages slow, deliberate eating. This involves chewing thoroughly, savoring the taste and texture of food, and allowing time for digestion. It gives your body time to register fullness and send appropriate signals to the brain to cease eating, preventing overeating. It also involves eating without distractions such as televisions, smartphones, or computers. These distractions can lead to mechanical eating where food is consumed without awareness, leading to overeating. Being present and aware during meals allows us to derive more satisfaction from less food, thus aiding weight management.

Equally important in mindful eating is understanding the emotional relationship with food. Many people turn to food as a source of comfort or distraction in times of stress, anxiety, or boredom – a phenomenon known as emotional eating. By bringing awareness to these patterns, one can learn to respond to emotional cues with non-food related strategies, thus breaking the cycle of emotional eating. Moreover, mindful eating promotes a non-judgmental approach to food. It shifts the focus from labeling foods as 'good' or 'bad' to understanding the nutritional value of foods and their impact on the body. This allows for a healthier relationship with food, free of guilt or anxiety. Incorporating mindful eating into your daily routine doesn't require drastic changes. It can start with something as simple as paying more attention to the food you're eating at your next meal. As you progress, you may find yourself naturally gravitating towards healthier food choices, portion sizes that match your hunger, and better responses to emotional triggers. While mindful eating may seem simple, its effects can be profound.

Studies suggest that it can help manage weight, reduce binge eating, and improve blood sugar control – all critical aspects of managing and preventing diabetes. Therefore, mindful eating can be a valuable addition to a comprehensive diabetes management plan, complementing dietary changes, regular exercise, and medication. It's important to remember that mindful eating is a practice that develops over time. It's not about achieving perfection but about making incremental changes that enhance awareness and improve health. In a world where we're often disconnected from our bodies and our food, mindful eating offers a way to reconnect and cultivate a healthier, more balanced approach to nutrition. It invites us to bring the same attention to eating that we do to other important aspects of our lives, and in doing so, improve our health and wellbeing.

Benefits of Mindful Eating for Diabetics

Incorporating mindful eating into one's lifestyle can be particularly beneficial for individuals with diabetes or those at risk. Diabetes management is often tightly linked with dietary habits, making mindful eating a crucial aspect of comprehensive diabetes care. The beneficial impacts of mindful eating on individuals with diabetes are manifold, and these benefits can significantly contribute to overall health and well-being. One of the major benefits of mindful eating for diabetics is its potential to help regulate blood sugar levels. Mindful eating encourages individuals to eat only when they're truly hungry and to stop when they're full, reducing the likelihood of overeating. Overeating, especially foods high in sugar or carbohydrates, can result in a surge in blood sugar levels. By promoting conscious eating, mindful eating helps in regulating meal portions and timing, thus contributing to better blood sugar management. Furthermore, mindful eating helps in weight management. Obesity or excess weight is a significant risk factor for type 2 diabetes, and weight loss is often recommended for individuals with diabetes or prediabetes. As mindful eating helps to prevent overeating and encourages healthier food choices, it can be an effective tool in managing weight.

A meta-analysis of mindful eating interventions showed consistent reductions in weight and body mass index (BMI), further emphasizing its role in weight management. Mindful eating also promotes healthy food choices. By eating mindfully, you're more likely to savor your food, which can make healthy food more satisfying. Over time, this can lead to a natural preference for healthier foods that support diabetes management, like whole grains, lean proteins, fruits, and vegetables. By focusing on the sensory experience of eating, mindful eating can help shift preferences away from processed or high-sugar foods towards more nutritious options. Another significant benefit of mindful eating is its ability to improve psychological well-being. Diabetes can often lead to feelings of stress and depression. Moreover, the dietary restrictions required for diabetes management can cause anxiety around food.

Mindful eating can help manage these feelings by reducing stress, increasing acceptance, and improving one's relationship with food. It encourages a non-judgmental approach to eating, which can alleviate food-related anxiety and guilt. Lastly, mindful eating contributes to a better understanding of hunger and satiety cues. This awareness is crucial for individuals with diabetes as it helps distinguish physical hunger from emotional hunger, reducing the likelihood of emotional eating. Emotional eating, which involves consuming food in response to emotions rather than hunger, can be detrimental to diabetes management as it often involves overeating or eating unhealthy food. In summary, mindful eating offers an array of benefits for individuals with diabetes. By encouraging a healthier relationship with food, it can help manage blood sugar levels, contribute to weight loss, promote healthier food choices, improve psychological well-being, and enhance the understanding of hunger and satiety cues.

However, it's important to note that mindful eating is not a stand-alone solution for diabetes management but a component of a holistic approach that includes a balanced diet, regular exercise, medication, and regular health check-ups. By incorporating mindful eating into a comprehensive diabetes management plan, individuals with diabetes can improve their health outcomes and overall quality of life.

Chapter 9: Eating Out With Diabetes

Strategies for Making Healthy Choices at Restaurants

Eating out at restaurants can often present a challenge for individuals managing diabetes. Restaurant meals are typically high in calories, sodium, and unhealthy fats, all of which can have a negative impact on blood sugar control and overall health. However, with mindful planning and strategic decision-making, it's entirely possible to enjoy restaurant meals while still adhering to a diabetes-friendly diet. The first step is to plan ahead. Many restaurants provide their menu online. Review the menu beforehand to identify the healthier options and make a preliminary choice.

This way, you're less likely to make impulsive, less healthy decisions when you're at the restaurant. When selecting dishes, opt for grilled, roasted, or steamed items instead of fried or sautéed ones. These cooking methods typically use less fat and thus reduce the calorie content of the meal. Moreover, dishes described as "creamy," "crispy," or "battered" often indicate high levels of fat and calories. Another strategy is to control portion sizes. Restaurant portions are often much larger than standard servings, leading to excessive calorie intake. Consider asking for a half-portion, sharing a meal with someone else, or packing half of your meal to go before you start eating.

This way, you're less likely to eat more than you intended out of a desire not to waste food. When it comes to sides, choose vegetables or salad over French fries or onion rings. However, be mindful of dressings and sauces which can add significant amounts of fat and calories. Ask for these on the side, so you can control the quantity. Also, it's essential to consider the type of cuisine. Some types of cuisine tend to be healthier than others. For example, Mediterranean cuisine is renowned for its emphasis on fruits, vegetables, lean proteins, and healthy fats. Similarly, Japanese cuisine often offers an array of seafood and vegetable options. That said, even within healthier cuisines, it's important to make conscious choices and control portion sizes. It's also crucial to monitor your carbohydrate intake. Be mindful of the bread basket and limit consumption of rice, pasta, and other carbohydrate-rich sides. Choose whole-grain options whenever possible. If you're ordering a sandwich or a burger, consider going "bunless" or ask for lettuce wraps instead. Beverage choices also matter. Sodas, sweet teas, and alcoholic beverages can significantly increase your blood sugar levels. Opt for water, unsweetened tea, or other non-caloric beverages. If you choose to drink alcohol, do so in moderation and never on an empty stomach. Lastly, communicate your dietary needs to the restaurant staff.

Most restaurants are accommodating of dietary restrictions and can modify dishes to meet your needs. Don't hesitate to ask about the ingredients or the cooking method of a dish. Eating out should be an enjoyable experience, and with these strategies, it can be both enjoyable and healthy. Remember, the goal isn't perfection but making better choices more often. With careful planning and smart decision-making, you can maintain your diabetes management goals while still enjoying the social and culinary pleasures of dining out.

What to Eat and Avoid

Eating healthfully with diabetes does not necessarily mean deprivation or completely eliminating certain foods from your diet. Instead, it's about making conscious, informed decisions that prioritize nutrient-dense foods and avoid or limit those that can adversely affect blood glucose levels and overall health. In terms of what to eat, focus on a variety of nutrient-dense, minimally processed foods.

Whole Grains: Whole grains are a great source of complex carbohydrates, fiber, and essential nutrients. They have a lower glycemic index compared to refined grains, meaning they cause a slower, more steady rise in blood sugar levels. Examples include whole wheat, brown rice, quinoa, oats, and whole grain pasta.

Lean Proteins: Proteins are essential for body repair and maintenance. Opt for lean protein sources, such as skinless chicken, turkey, fish, eggs, tofu, and lean cuts of meat. Plant-based protein sources like beans, lentils, and chickpeas are also excellent choices, providing fiber along with protein.

Fruits and Vegetables: Fruits and vegetables are packed with essential vitamins, minerals, fiber, and antioxidants. Aim for a colorful variety, as different colors indicate different nutrients. Opt for whole fruits instead of fruit juices to benefit from the fiber and limit rapid spikes in blood glucose.

Healthy Fats: Healthy fats, such as monounsaturated and polyunsaturated fats, can help lower levels of "bad" LDL cholesterol and increase "good" HDL cholesterol. Sources include avocados, nuts, seeds, olives, and fatty fish like salmon and mackerel.

Non-Starchy Vegetables: Non-starchy vegetables like broccoli, spinach, peppers, and cucumbers have fewer carbs than starchy vegetables like potatoes and corn. This makes them a good choice for people with diabetes. As for what to avoid or limit:

Refined Grains: Refined grains, like white bread and white rice, have had most of their fiber and nutrients removed. They can lead to rapid spikes in blood sugar and should be limited. Saturated and Trans Fats: Saturated and trans fats can raise your "bad" LDL cholesterol and lower your "good" HDL cholesterol, increasing your risk of heart disease. These are typically found in processed foods, fatty cuts of meat, full-fat dairy products, and fried foods.

Sugary Drinks: Sugary drinks, such as sodas, fruit punches, and sweetened coffees, can cause rapid increases in blood sugar and provide little nutritional value. They should be replaced with water, unsweetened tea, or other sugar-free beverages.

Processed Foods: Processed foods often contain unhealthy fats, added sugars, and high levels of sodium. They can also be low in fiber and essential nutrients, making them poor nutritional choices. Incorporating a variety of nutrient-dense foods into your diet and limiting or avoiding those that can negatively affect your blood glucose and overall health is key to managing diabetes. By making informed choices, you can enjoy a diverse, satisfying, and flavorful diet while also maintaining optimal blood sugar control.

Dealing with Social Gatherings

Social gatherings, events, and celebrations often pose a unique set of challenges for individuals managing diabetes. The abundance of food, especially dishes high in carbohydrates and sugars, can make blood glucose management seem daunting. However, with some planning, mindfulness, and assertiveness, you can successfully navigate these social settings. Firstly, planning is crucial. Knowing what to expect in terms of food can help you adjust your meal plan or medication regimen accordingly. If possible, inquire about the menu beforehand or offer to bring a dish that fits within your dietary guidelines. By preparing a healthy, diabetic-friendly dish, you ensure that there's at least one option you can enjoy without worry. Next, don't skip meals before the event to "save" carbs or calories for later. This strategy can lead to unstable blood sugar levels and overeating. Instead, eat your regular meals and snacks throughout the day to maintain stable blood sugar levels. When you arrive at the event, you'll be less likely to overindulge due to hunger.

Thirdly, practice portion control. With a variety of foods available, it's easy to overconsume without realizing it. To manage this, start by filling half of your plate with non-starchy vegetables, one quarter with lean protein, and one quarter with carbohydrates. This ensures a balanced meal that won't drastically spike your blood sugar levels. Another crucial aspect is monitoring your alcohol consumption. Alcohol can affect blood sugar levels and interact with diabetes medications. If you choose to drink, do so in moderation and never on an empty stomach.

The American Diabetes Association recommends up to one drink per day for women and up to two drinks per day for men, with one drink equivalent to a 12-ounce beer, 5-ounce glass of wine, or 1.5 ounces of distilled spirits. Communicating your needs is also vital. Don't hesitate to let hosts or waitstaff know about your dietary needs. Being open about your condition can help others understand your choices and even offer support.

Last but not least, monitor your blood sugar. Social events can disrupt your normal routine and diet, so it's essential to monitor your blood sugar levels more closely. Regular testing can help you understand how different foods and the overall excitement of the event impact your blood sugar levels. While social gatherings may pose challenges, they are also opportunities to enjoy food and fellowship. With planning, mindfulness, and assertiveness, you can successfully navigate social events while keeping your diabetes management on track. Remember that it's okay to enjoy the occasion; diabetes management is not about perfection, but about achieving a balance that allows you to live a healthy, satisfying life.

Chapter 10: Exercise and Diabetes

The Role of Physical Activity in Managing Diabetes

Regular physical activity plays an indispensable role in managing diabetes. It assists in maintaining a healthy weight, reducing blood glucose levels, improving insulin sensitivity, and enhancing overall cardiovascular health. It is no exaggeration to say that engaging in regular exercise is one of the most effective ways to manage diabetes and improve the quality of life. Regular exercise promotes weight management, an essential aspect of diabetes control. Maintaining a healthy body weight can significantly reduce the risk of developing complications related to diabetes, including heart disease and stroke. Exercise burns calories and builds muscle, both of which contribute to weight control. It's worth noting that even modest weight loss can improve insulin sensitivity and glycemic control. A remarkable benefit of exercise for people with diabetes is its direct impact on blood glucose levels. Physical activity encourages muscles to use glucose for energy, thereby lowering blood sugar levels in the body. This effect can last for hours or even up to a day or more after the activity, depending on the intensity and duration of the exercise.

Next, physical activity also increases insulin sensitivity, which means your body's insulin works more effectively. This is crucial because better insulin sensitivity can lead to lower blood glucose levels after meals and less need for medication. Engaging in regular exercise also provides substantial cardiovascular benefits. Diabetes increases the risk of heart disease and stroke, and physical activity strengthens the heart, lowers blood pressure, improves circulation, and reduces cholesterol levels, all of which contribute to better heart health. There are various forms of physical activities suitable for individuals with diabetes. Aerobic exercises, such as walking, swimming, or biking, enhance your heart rate and work large muscle groups.

These types of exercises help to reduce insulin resistance and improve heart health. Resistance or strength training exercises, such as lifting weights or using resistance bands, help build muscle mass. Greater muscle mass improves metabolic rate and helps your body use insulin more effectively. It also aids in maintaining healthy body composition, which is crucial for managing diabetes. Remember, it's crucial to monitor your blood glucose levels before, during, and after exercise to prevent hypoglycemia, a condition characterized by abnormally low blood sugar levels. This is especially important if you are taking insulin or medications that can lower your blood sugar. Always consult your healthcare provider before starting a new exercise regimen.

They can guide you to choose safe and suitable activities that take into account your overall health, fitness level, and specific needs related to diabetes management. In conclusion, physical activity is not just a cornerstone but a pillar of diabetes management. It's an essential part of a holistic approach to managing diabetes, alongside diet and medication. Regular physical activity not only helps manage diabetes but also contributes significantly to overall health and well-being. It empowers individuals with diabetes to live active, fulfilling lives without letting their condition hinder them.

Exercise Guidelines for People with Diabetes

For individuals living with diabetes, adhering to exercise guidelines can make a significant difference in managing the condition. These guidelines are not merely suggestions but carefully thought-out recommendations designed to provide safe and effective ways to incorporate physical activity into daily routines. A multi-faceted approach to exercise, tailored to the individual's specific needs and capabilities, is the key to successful diabetes management. The American Diabetes Association (ADA) suggests that individuals with diabetes should aim for a minimum of 150 minutes per week of moderate-to-vigorous aerobic activity. This can be achieved by exercising for 30 minutes a day, five days a week. Moderate aerobic exercises can include activities like brisk walking, dancing, swimming, or biking. In addition to aerobic exercises, the ADA also recommends performing resistance training at least twice a week. Resistance training can include lifting weights, using resistance bands, or performing bodyweight exercises like push-ups and squats. These types of activities increase muscle strength and improve insulin sensitivity, both of which can help control blood glucose levels. When designing an exercise program, it's important to consider various factors such as the type of diabetes, the presence of any diabetes-related complications, the individual's age, and current level of fitness. Consulting with a healthcare provider or a certified diabetes educator can provide valuable insight into designing a suitable and safe exercise regimen. For those who are new to exercise, it's important to start slowly and gradually increase the intensity and duration of workouts.

This can help prevent injuries and make the transition to a more active lifestyle more manageable. A short walk after meals, for instance, can be a great way to begin. It's also crucial to incorporate warm-up and cool-down periods into each workout. A warm-up of five to ten minutes helps prepare the body for exercise by gradually increasing the heart rate, while a cool-down helps return the heart rate to its resting state. It's also essential to stay hydrated during exercise and avoid exercising in extreme temperatures, which can lead to dehydration and impact blood sugar levels. Those who are taking insulin or medications that lower blood sugar should monitor their glucose levels before, during, and after exercise to prevent hypoglycemia.

Furthermore, people with diabetes should always wear a medical ID that identifies their condition in case of an emergency. It is also advisable to carry a carbohydrate snack in case blood sugar levels drop too low during exercise. In conclusion, regular physical activity is an essential component of diabetes management. Following these guidelines can provide a roadmap for incorporating exercise into a daily routine safely and effectively. But remember, every person is unique, and what works for one person might not work for another. It's important to find physical activities that are enjoyable, fit into your lifestyle, and meet your personal health goals. Exercise, along with proper nutrition and medication, if necessary, can help individuals with diabetes lead a healthy and active life.

Building a Personalized Exercise Plan

Constructing a personalized exercise plan can be a vital component in effectively managing diabetes. It enables individuals to tailor their physical activities to their specific needs, abilities, preferences, and goals, ensuring that the regimen is not only beneficial for their health but also sustainable in the long term. Here's how to go about building a personalized exercise plan. Firstly, it's essential to establish clear, achievable fitness goals. Whether it's improving blood glucose control, losing weight, or increasing physical strength, having defined objectives can provide a sense of purpose and direction. These goals should be SMART: Specific, Measurable, Attainable, Relevant, and Time-bound. A fitness goal might be something like: "I will walk for 30 minutes a day, five days a week, for the next four weeks." This goal is specific (walking), measurable (30 minutes), attainable and relevant (considering the person's ability and the ADA's exercise guidelines), and time-bound (four weeks). Secondly, selecting enjoyable activities is key to maintaining an exercise routine.

If a person dreads their workouts, they're less likely to stick with them in the long run. Whether it's dancing, swimming, biking, yoga, or even gardening, choose activities that are enjoyable and fit into the lifestyle. Next, determining the frequency, duration, and intensity of the exercises is crucial. This should be guided by the ADA's recommendations, personal fitness goals, and the healthcare provider's advice. As a general guideline, most people with diabetes should aim for a minimum of 150 minutes of moderate-to-vigorous aerobic activity per week, supplemented by resistance training twice a week.

A well-rounded exercise plan should include a variety of activities. It's beneficial to have a mix of aerobic exercises (for cardiovascular health and blood glucose control), resistance or strength training (for muscle strength and insulin sensitivity), and flexibility exercises (for joint health and range of motion). It's equally important to build in time for recovery. Rest days allow the body to recuperate and adapt to the physical stress of exercise. Overdoing it can lead to burnout and increase the risk of injuries. Consistent monitoring of blood glucose levels before, during, and after exercise is crucial to assess how different activities affect blood glucose and to avoid hypoglycemia. This information can be used to make necessary adjustments to the exercise routine or diabetes management plan. Furthermore, planning for challenges can set the stage for successful diabetes management. This can include figuring out strategies for dealing with bad weather (like having indoor workout options), managing time constraints, or coping with periods of illness or stress. Lastly, seeking professional guidance can be immensely helpful, especially when starting out.

A fitness professional, preferably with experience in working with people with diabetes, can provide valuable input in designing a safe and effective exercise plan. Remember, the most effective exercise plan is the one that's followed. Starting slowly, setting realistic goals, and focusing on progress rather than perfection can make the journey towards better health enjoyable and rewarding. A personalized exercise plan, combined with proper nutrition and diabetes medication (if needed), can help individuals with diabetes lead active, healthy lives. Always consult a healthcare provider before beginning any new exercise regimen.

EXAMPLE OF WORKOUT: Here's a simple 30-day home exercise plan designed for individuals with diabetes, taking into account the ADA's recommendations for physical activity. The plan includes three workouts per week – let's designate them for Mondays, Wednesdays, and Fridays, but they can be adapted to fit personal schedules. Before you start, make sure to consult your healthcare provider. This program focuses on bodyweight exercises, which can be performed without special tools or machines. If you have a yoga mat, it could be useful but is not strictly necessary.

Week 1: Getting Started

- Monday: Start with a warm-up by marching in place for 5 minutes. Follow this with 10 minutes of full body stretching exercises. End the session with a 5-minute cooldown of slow walking around the house.

- Wednesday: Repeat Monday's routine, but after the warm-up and stretching, add in 5 minutes of standing leg lifts (alternate legs).

- Friday: Repeat Wednesday's routine, but add 5 minutes of seated leg extensions (alternate legs) after the leg lifts.

Week 2: Building Strength

- Monday: After the warm-up and stretching, do 10 minutes of chair squats and wall push-ups (5 sets of each, alternating, with a break in between sets).

- Wednesday: Repeat Monday's routine, but replace wall push-ups with standing leg lifts.

- Friday: Repeat Wednesday's routine, but add 5 minutes of seated leg extensions after the leg lifts.

Week 3: Increasing Intensity

- Monday: After the warm-up and stretching, do 15 minutes of chair squats and wall push-ups (5 sets of each, alternating, with a break in between sets).

- Wednesday: Repeat Monday's routine, but replace wall push-ups with standing leg lifts.

- Friday: Repeat Wednesday's routine, but add 5 minutes of seated leg extensions after the leg lifts.

Week 4: Maintaining Consistency

- Monday: After the warm-up and stretching, do 15 minutes of chair squats, wall push-ups, standing leg lifts, and seated leg extensions (5 sets of each, alternating, with a break in between sets).

- Wednesday: Repeat Monday's routine.
- Friday: Repeat Monday's routine. Remember to always listen to your body and adjust the intensity of the workouts according to how you feel.

The plan is flexible, so feel free to switch days or exercises if necessary. Keep monitoring your blood glucose levels before and after exercise. Drink plenty of water, take breaks as needed, and enjoy the process of getting healthier!

Note: Chair squats are performed by standing in front of a chair and lowering your body as if you were about to sit down, then standing back up. Wall push-ups are done by standing an arm's length away from a wall, placing your hands on the wall at chest height, and then bending and straightening your arms. Standing leg lifts involve lifting one leg to the side or back while standing, holding onto a wall or chair for balance. Seated leg extensions are done by sitting on a chair, extending one leg out straight, and then lowering it back down

Chapter 11: Medication and Insulin Management

Understanding Your Medication

Medication forms a crucial pillar in the management of diabetes alongside diet and physical activity. It's essential to have a comprehensive understanding of your prescribed medications, including their function, dosage, timing, and potential side effects. There are several classes of drugs that are utilized in diabetes management, each with a specific mechanism of action to control blood glucose levels. The first line of treatment for type 2 diabetes is often metformin, a biguanide. This drug works by reducing the amount of glucose released by the liver and improving insulin sensitivity, thereby facilitating glucose uptake by the body's cells. Another class of medications is sulfonylureas, such as glipizide and glyburide. These function by stimulating the pancreas to release more insulin. Meanwhile, DPP-4 inhibitors, like sitagliptin and saxagliptin, block the action of DPP-4 enzymes, thus prolonging the action of incretin hormones which stimulate insulin release in response to a meal.

Thiazolidinediones, like pioglitazone and rosiglitazone, work by increasing the body's sensitivity to insulin, allowing more glucose to be absorbed into cells. SGLT2 inhibitors, such as empagliflozin and canagliflozin, block the reabsorption of glucose in the kidneys, causing excess glucose to be excreted in the urine. For type 1 diabetes and advanced stages of type 2 diabetes, insulin therapy becomes necessary. There are different types of insulin available, varying in onset and duration of action. Rapid-acting insulin starts to work within 15 minutes of injection, peaking at approximately 1 hour, and continues to work for 2 to 4 hours. Regular or short-acting insulin usually reaches the bloodstream within 30 minutes of injection, peaks anywhere from 2 to 3 hours after injection, and is effective for approximately 3 to 6 hours.

Intermediate-acting insulin generally reaches the bloodstream about 2 to 4 hours after injection, peaks 4 to 12 hours later, and is effective for about 12 to 18 hours. Long-acting insulin reaches the bloodstream several hours after injection and tends to lower glucose levels fairly evenly over a 24-hour period. Being knowledgeable about your prescribed medication involves more than just recognizing their names. Understanding the dosage is equally important. Diabetes medications often require careful titration and frequent adjustments to maintain optimal blood glucose control. Knowing when to take your medication is also crucial. Some drugs are taken before meals to control postprandial (after meal) blood sugar spikes, while others are taken once or twice daily irrespective of meal timings. Awareness of potential side effects is another essential aspect.

Most diabetes medications are well-tolerated, but they can cause side effects ranging from minor issues like nausea or upset stomach to more severe ones like hypoglycemia (low blood sugar) or kidney problems. It's vital to remember that medication is not a substitute for a healthy lifestyle. Instead, it complements dietary changes and regular physical activity in managing diabetes. Always consult your healthcare provider or pharmacist if you have any questions or concerns about your medication. They can provide detailed information tailored to your specific situation and needs, ensuring the most effective use of medication in your diabetes management plan.

Insulin: What You Need to Know

Insulin, a hormone produced by the pancreas, plays an essential role in regulating blood glucose levels. In individuals with diabetes, the body either doesn't produce enough insulin (type 1 diabetes), or it doesn't use the insulin effectively (type 2 diabetes). As a result, glucose builds up in the blood, leading to high blood sugar levels. When diet, physical activity, and oral medications are not enough to manage blood glucose, insulin therapy becomes necessary. Understanding the different types, dosages, administration methods, and possible side effects of insulin is crucial for those who rely on this medication for glucose regulation. There are several types of insulin, categorized based on how quickly they start to work (onset), when they peak, and how long they continue to work (duration).

1. **Rapid-acting insulin** begins to work about 15 minutes after injection, peaks around 1 hour after injection, and continues to work for 2 to 4 hours. This type includes insulin lispro (Humalog), insulin aspart (NovoLog), and insulin glulisine (Apidra).

2. **Short-acting insulin** reaches the bloodstream within 30 minutes of injection, peaks around 2 to 3 hours after injection, and is effective for approximately 3 to 6 hours. Regular (R) insulin, such as Humulin R and Novolin R, falls into this category.

3. **Intermediate-acting insulin** reaches the bloodstream about 2 to 4 hours after injection, peaks 4 to 12 hours later, and is effective for about 12 to 18 hours. NPH (N) insulin, such as Humulin N and Novolin N, are examples of this type.

4. **Long-acting insulin** has a slow, steady release and lowers glucose levels fairly evenly over a 24-hour period. This category includes insulin glargine (Lantus) and insulin detemir (Levemir).

5. **Ultra-long-acting insulin** works consistently for over 24 hours, with no noticeable peak. Insulin degludec (Tresiba) is one example of this type.

Another critical aspect of insulin therapy is the method of administration. Insulin can't be taken orally because stomach enzymes would break it down, rendering it ineffective. Therefore, it's typically injected under the skin using a fine needle and syringe, an insulin pen, or an insulin pump. Correct dosage is crucial in insulin therapy. Overdosing can lead to hypoglycemia (low blood sugar), a condition that can cause symptoms such as shakiness, sweating, confusion, and in severe cases, loss of consciousness.

Conversely, not using enough insulin can result in hyperglycemia (high blood sugar), leading to symptoms such as frequent urination, increased thirst, fatigue, and blurry vision. Storing insulin correctly is also of utmost importance. Most types of insulin need to be refrigerated before opening but can be kept at room temperature after they're opened. However, they should not be exposed to extreme temperatures. Potential side effects of insulin therapy can include weight gain, allergic reactions, and lipodystrophy (changes in fat tissue at the injection site). Hypoglycemia, as previously mentioned, can also occur. Despite these challenges, insulin therapy is a lifeline for many people with diabetes. Understanding how it works, how to administer it, and how to handle potential problems is essential for maintaining optimal blood sugar control. As with all aspects of diabetes management, the key is to work closely with your healthcare provider to adjust your treatment plan as needed, taking into consideration your lifestyle, health status, and treatment goals.

Safe and Effective Medication Practices

Effective diabetes management requires an understanding of how to safely use medications, both to control blood sugar levels and to manage any comorbid conditions often seen with diabetes. This includes understanding the mechanism of action, the correct dosages, the timing of medication, possible side effects, and how different medications may interact with each other. The correct dosage of medication is a critical aspect of safe use. The prescribed amount of medication should always be adhered to. Changes to the dosage should only be made in consultation with a healthcare professional. Taking too much medication can lead to side effects or toxicities, while taking too little can make the medication ineffective. Timing of medication is equally important, particularly with diabetes drugs. Some diabetes medications need to be taken before, during, or after meals to work effectively. For instance, rapid-acting insulin should be taken just before or after meals, while long-acting insulin is usually taken at the same time each day, regardless of meals.

Understanding the potential side effects and adverse reactions of medications is necessary. Most medications come with a patient information leaflet that provides comprehensive details about the drug. However, it's also important to discuss potential side effects with your healthcare provider. Common side effects can include gastrointestinal problems, weight changes, hypoglycemia (low blood sugar), and skin reactions at injection sites for those on insulin therapy. Being aware of drug interactions is crucial, as some drugs can interfere with the efficacy of diabetes medications or cause harmful side effects. For instance, certain blood pressure medications, like thiazide diuretics, can increase blood sugar levels, while some cholesterol-lowering drugs may interact with blood sugar control medications. Inform your healthcare provider of all the medications you're taking, including over-the-counter drugs and dietary supplements, to ensure there's no potential for adverse interactions. In addition to these practices, storing medications correctly can impact their effectiveness.

Many diabetes medications, including insulin, need to be stored under specific conditions. Insulin, for instance, should be stored in the refrigerator before opening, but it can be kept at room temperature after opening, as long as it's away from extreme heat and light. Regular monitoring of blood sugar levels is vital when taking diabetes medication. It helps to assess the efficacy of the treatment and guides any necessary changes to the medication regimen. In essence, the safety and effectiveness of medication practices hinge on a comprehensive understanding of your prescribed medications, regular communication with your healthcare provider, and adherence to the medication regimen. It's a delicate balance that, when managed well, can significantly improve the quality of life for those living with diabetes. As always, the approach to medication should be personalized, considering the unique needs and circumstances of each individual. It's essential to make regular appointments with your healthcare provider to review and adjust your medication regimen as needed, ensuring optimal blood sugar control and overall health. Indeed, when it comes to administering insulin, individuals with diabetes should follow certain rules and practices that can aid in effective management and facilitate their daily life, reducing worries and promoting confidence.

Let's delve into some practical tips and examples. Firstly, one must know when to take insulin. This primarily depends on the type of insulin prescribed. For instance, rapid-acting insulin is taken around meal times, either just before, during, or immediately after eating. Long-acting insulin is typically administered once or twice a day, irrespective of meals. Therefore, being aware of the type of insulin and its corresponding timing is critical. Always carry your insulin with you, especially if you are going out for meals or work. Secondly, insulin administration requires attention to injection sites. The abdomen, thighs, buttocks, and upper arms are the common sites. Regularly rotating the injection site within the same region can prevent tissue damage and ensure better absorption of insulin. Let's envision some daily life scenarios: At home: Make it a habit to administer insulin at the same place and time each day. This will not only help remember to take the dose but also ensure the medication is stored correctly. A well-lit room with a table and a chair will provide a comfortable place for insulin injection. Always clean the injection site with an alcohol swab and let it air-dry before injecting. At work: Keep your insulin and supplies in a cool, dry place.

If your job involves physical labor, try to inject insulin in an area not affected by muscle movements. Schedule your insulin doses around your meal breaks, if possible. In restaurants: Try to estimate the carbohydrate content of your meal, and adjust your insulin dose accordingly. If you take insulin before meals, time your injection so that you're not waiting long before your food arrives. If the wait time is unpredictable, consider using rapid-acting insulin after your meal. A trip to the restroom can provide privacy for your injection. While traveling: Always carry extra supplies of insulin and needles/syringes or insulin pen. Bring along a letter from your healthcare provider explaining your need for insulin and supplies. If you are flying, keep your insulin in your carry-on bag to prevent it from getting too cold in the checked baggage.

Social gatherings: If you're at a party, you might not know when food will be served. In such cases, it's often best to take a dose of rapid-acting insulin after you eat, rather than before. This allows for flexibility in timing and can help avoid a potential hypoglycemic episode if mealtime is delayed. Administering insulin effectively requires knowledge, practice, and a bit of strategic planning. Over time, as you gain confidence, managing your insulin regimen will become an integrated part of your life. Remember, if you ever feel unsure or concerned about any aspect of your insulin use, always consult your healthcare provider or a diabetes educator. They can provide personal guidance tailored to your needs and lifestyle.

Chapter 12: Monitoring Blood Sugar Levels

How to Monitor Your Blood Sugar Levels

Blood glucose monitoring is an integral part of diabetes management. It provides essential information about your current blood sugar levels, helps identify patterns and trends, and informs decision-making regarding medication, diet, and physical activity. It also enables you to prevent or detect high (hyperglycemia) and low (hypoglycemia) blood glucose levels. To effectively monitor your blood glucose, it's crucial to understand how to perform a blood glucose test correctly, when and how often to test, and what the results mean.

Performing a Blood Glucose Test

The process of blood glucose testing involves several steps. Initially, gather all your supplies: a glucose meter, a test strip, a lancet device for pricking your finger, and a clean tissue or cloth. The glucose meter is an electronic device that measures and displays your blood sugar level. A test strip is a small strip that is inserted into the glucose meter and is used to apply the blood sample. A lancet device is a small instrument with a sharp needle to prick your finger. To start the test, wash your hands with warm soapy water, rinse thoroughly, and dry them. Insert the test strip into the glucose meter. Prick the side of your finger (not the tip) with the lancet device. You might need to adjust the depth setting on the device to get a large enough blood sample. Gently squeeze your finger to obtain a drop of blood. Apply the drop of blood to the end of the test strip. The glucose meter will take a few seconds to display the reading.

When and How Often to Test

The frequency and timing of glucose monitoring depend on the type of diabetes, the nature of your treatment plan, your blood glucose control, and your individual healthcare provider's recommendations. Here are some general guidelines:

1. People with type 1 diabetes who use insulin often test their blood sugar levels four or more times per day, typically before meals and snacks, occasionally after eating, at bedtime, before physical activity, when they suspect low blood sugar, and before critical tasks such as driving.

2. Individuals with type 2 diabetes often test less frequently, but the timing can vary. Some may need to test only once a day, while others might need to check it three or four times a day.

Understanding the Results

Blood glucose meter readings provide a snapshot of your blood sugar level at the moment of testing. The target range for most people, according to the American Diabetes Association, is between 80 to 130 mg/dL before meals and less than 180 mg/dL two hours after meals. But remember, the optimal range can vary depending on individual factors and your healthcare provider's advice. Persistent readings above or below your target range can be an indicator of a problem and warrant a discussion with your healthcare provider. It's essential to keep a record of your blood sugar readings, including the date, time, and any influencing factors like meals, physical activity, stress, or illness. While self-monitoring of blood glucose provides immediate information about your blood sugar levels, it doesn't provide a comprehensive picture of your glucose control over time. The A1C test, which is performed by a healthcare provider, measures your average blood sugar level over the past 2 to 3 months.

Together, both types of tests provide a more complete view of your blood glucose control. Blood glucose monitoring is not just about collecting data. The true value lies in using this information to improve your self-care and decision-making skills. The patterns you notice, the choices you make, and the improvements you see all contribute to managing diabetes more effectively and confidently.

Understanding Your Blood Sugar

Readings Understanding your blood sugar readings and knowing what to do based on them is a vital aspect of diabetes management. Blood glucose values can give you and your healthcare team insights into how well your diabetes care plan is working and can provide direction for adjustments when necessary. It can guide decision-making in relation to diet, physical activity, and medication, and assist in preventing or managing hyperglycemia (high blood sugar) and hypoglycemia (low blood sugar). Firstly, let's discuss what normal, low, and high blood glucose levels are. Normal fasting blood sugar levels, for someone without diabetes, range from 70 to 99 milligrams per deciliter (mg/dL). For a person with diabetes, the American Diabetes Association recommends a target fasting or pre-meal blood sugar level of 80 to 130 mg/dL.

Postprandial or after-meal levels should be less than 180 mg/dL, taken two hours after the start of a meal. Hypoglycemia is defined as a blood glucose level below 70 mg/dL. It can be caused by factors such as taking too much insulin or other diabetes medications, skipping a meal, or exercising harder than usual. Symptoms may include shaking, sweating, rapid heartbeat, headache, dizziness, and even fainting if not addressed promptly. On the other hand, hyperglycemia occurs when the blood glucose level is consistently higher than 180 mg/dL. It could be due to eating more than planned, being less active than usual, or under stress. Frequent urination, excessive thirst, fatigue, and blurred vision are among the signs of hyperglycemia. Now, let's illustrate this understanding with an example: Imagine a person named Sam, who is living with type 2 diabetes. He checks his blood glucose regularly four times a day: upon waking (fasting), before lunch, before dinner, and at bedtime.

One morning, Sam wakes up and checks his fasting blood sugar, and it reads 90 mg/dL. This is within the recommended range, so no adjustments are necessary. He eats a balanced breakfast, follows his regular medication routine, and carries on with his day. Before lunch, Sam checks his blood glucose again. This time it reads 130 mg/dL. This value is on the higher side of the normal pre-meal range, but still within target. He decides to take a short walk before eating lunch to help lower his blood glucose level. Before dinner, Sam checks his blood glucose, and it's 180 mg/dL. The reading is higher than the recommended pre-meal target. Looking back at his day, Sam realizes that his lunch was higher in carbohydrates than usual. He decides to have a low-carb dinner and plan for an after-dinner walk. At bedtime, Sam checks his blood sugar one last time, and it reads 140 mg/dL. Although this is a bit high, it's not alarmingly so. Sam knows that he will need to discuss this pattern with his healthcare provider if it continues.

In this example, Sam was able to make decisions about his meals and physical activity based on his blood sugar readings. He recognized when a reading was outside of the target range and took steps to correct it. Most importantly, Sam knows that he is not alone in managing his diabetes. He maintains regular communication with his healthcare provider and discusses his blood glucose patterns and any necessary changes to his diabetes care plan.

What to Do When Your Blood Sugar is Too High or Too Low

Managing blood sugar levels effectively is an integral part of living with diabetes. Occasionally, despite your best efforts, blood glucose levels might fall too low (hypoglycemia) or rise too high (hyperglycemia). Both situations warrant immediate action to prevent complications and restore balance. Let's delve into the appropriate response to these scenarios.

Managing Hypoglycemia

Hypoglycemia, characterized by a blood sugar level below 70 mg/dL, can be a scary experience. Common symptoms include shaking, sweating, confusion, blurred vision, and in severe cases, loss of consciousness. In these situations, it's crucial to act quickly. First, confirm hypoglycemia by checking your blood sugar if possible. Then, consume 15-20 grams of fast-acting carbohydrates. This could be glucose tablets or gel, fruit juice, non-diet soda, or even a tablespoon of honey or sugar. Recheck your blood sugar after 15 minutes. If it's still below 70 mg/dL, repeat the process until it's back within the normal range. Once your blood sugar stabilizes, if your next meal is more than an hour away, have a snack that includes protein and complex carbohydrates, such as a slice of whole grain bread with peanut butter.

Managing Hyperglycemia

On the other side of the spectrum is hyperglycemia, defined by a blood sugar level consistently higher than 180 mg/dL. Frequent urination, extreme thirst, and fatigue are among the symptoms. Persistent hyperglycemia can lead to severe complications such as diabetic ketoacidosis (DKA) or hyperglycemic hyperosmolar syndrome (HHS). If you have high blood sugar, drinking water can help flush excess sugar out of your system through urine. Light physical activity may also lower blood sugar, but only if your blood sugar is under 240 mg/dL and ketones are not present in your urine. It's important to monitor your blood sugar closely, retesting every few hours.

If hyperglycemia persists or if you experience symptoms of DKA (such as nausea, vomiting, abdominal pain, or fruity-smelling breath), seek medical attention immediately. If you're on insulin therapy, you may need to take an additional dose of insulin, but always consult your healthcare provider before making adjustments to your medication regimen. Consider the following example for a clearer understanding: Alex, a 35-year-old with type 1 diabetes, wakes up feeling tired and thirsty, despite drinking plenty of water the night before. He checks his blood glucose, which reads 250 mg/dL. Alex is aware that his blood glucose is too high. He drinks a few glasses of water and opts for a low-carb, high-protein breakfast.

He checks his urine for ketones using a test strip and finds that they are negative, indicating that his body isn't producing them as a response to lack of insulin. Alex decides to take a gentle walk, remembering that light activity can help lower blood glucose levels. He rechecks his blood glucose level after two hours, which has decreased to 220 mg/dL, still high but moving in the right direction. He continues to hydrate and avoids carbohydrates. By lunchtime, his blood glucose has dropped to 190 mg/dL. He continues his day as usual, maintaining regular monitoring and making necessary adjustments to his activity and food intake. However, he also knows that if his blood glucose doesn't return to a normal range, he should consult his healthcare provider for advice. Understanding and promptly responding to blood glucose fluctuations is critical in diabetes management. Being equipped with the right knowledge empowers you to take charge of your health, ultimately leading to improved outcomes and a better quality of life.

Chapter 13: Complementary and Alternative Therapies

Understanding Complementary and Alternative Therapies

Complementary and alternative medicine (CAM) has seen a surge in interest in recent years. While conventional treatments remain the cornerstone of diabetes management, some patients seek additional ways to improve their well-being and blood sugar control. This chapter will explore complementary and alternative therapies for diabetes, focusing on the science behind them, their potential benefits, and the need for consultation with healthcare professionals before trying new therapies.

Complementary and alternative therapies encompass a wide range of practices and products not considered part of conventional medicine. They are typically classified into two categories: "complementary" therapies, used alongside conventional treatments, and "alternative" therapies, used in place of conventional treatments.

Complementary Therapies

Complementary therapies for diabetes often focus on lifestyle modifications, dietary supplements, and mind-body practices. Here are some examples:

1. **Dietary Supplements**: Certain dietary supplements, such as cinnamon, alpha-lipoic acid, and chromium, have been studied for their potential to improve blood sugar control in diabetes. However, the results have been mixed, and more research is needed to establish their effectiveness and safety.

2. **Physical Activity**: Yoga and Tai Chi, with their combination of physical postures, breathing exercises, and meditation, may help enhance body awareness, reduce stress, and promote a sense of well-being. Some studies suggest that these practices

can also aid in blood sugar control and weight management, but additional research is needed.

3. **Mind-Body Practices**: Mindfulness-based stress reduction (MBSR) and other mindfulness practices can help individuals with diabetes cope with stress and anxiety, which can indirectly influence blood sugar control.

Alternative Therapies

Alternative therapies for diabetes typically involve treatments that are used instead of conventional medicine, often based on traditional healing systems. Examples include traditional Chinese medicine, Ayurveda, and homeopathy. However, it's important to note that no alternative therapies have been scientifically proven to cure diabetes or replace the need for insulin or other diabetes medications. While some people report improved well-being or symptom relief from these treatments, they should not be used as a substitute for proven, science-based medical treatments. Regardless of the type of therapy, the decision to use complementary or alternative treatments should always involve a discussion with your healthcare provider. While some treatments may offer potential benefits, others may have side effects, interact with your diabetes medications, or lead to inadequate control of blood sugar if used in place of standard treatments.

Your healthcare provider can help assess the safety and effectiveness of these treatments based on the latest scientific research and your personal health circumstances. For instance, consider the case of James, a 52-year-old with type 2 diabetes. He heard about the potential benefits of cinnamon for blood sugar control and was interested in trying it. Instead of starting the supplement on his own, James discussed his plans with his healthcare provider. After considering James' overall health, medication regimen, and the latest scientific evidence, they decided to integrate a controlled amount of cinnamon into his diet.

They also agreed on close monitoring of his blood sugar levels to assess the supplement's effect and ensure ongoing safety. Understanding complementary and alternative therapies for diabetes involves discerning between evidence-based practices and those with insufficient scientific backing. This knowledge, coupled with ongoing dialogue with healthcare providers, ensures that you can safely explore a wide array of options for managing your diabetes and improving your quality of life.

Evidence for Use in Diabetes Management

As more people express interest in complementary and alternative therapies for managing their diabetes, it's crucial to understand the evidence behind these treatments. This chapter will delve into the scientific data regarding the efficacy and safety of some widely used complementary and alternative therapies in diabetes management.

Dietary Supplements

A variety of dietary supplements are used by individuals with diabetes with the hope of improving their blood sugar control. For instance, chromium supplements have been studied due to the role of chromium in carbohydrate metabolism. Some studies have suggested a modest improvement in blood glucose control with chromium supplementation, particularly for people with poor baseline control. However, many of these studies have methodological limitations, and larger, more rigorous trials have generally not shown a benefit. Therefore, the routine use of chromium for blood glucose control cannot be recommended based on the current evidence. Cinnamon has also been examined for its potential antidiabetic effects.

While some small studies have shown improved blood glucose and cholesterol levels in people with type 2 diabetes using cinnamon, other well-conducted trials have failed to show any benefit.

Thus, while cinnamon is generally safe when used in culinary amounts, its use as a treatment for improving diabetes control is not supported by strong scientific evidence.

Physical Activities

Physical activities like yoga and Tai Chi have been associated with a range of health benefits, including improved blood sugar control, weight management, and mental well-being. Research has suggested that yoga can improve glycemic control, lipid levels, and body composition in individuals with type 2 diabetes. Similarly, some studies have shown benefits of Tai Chi for diabetes management, including improved blood glucose, blood pressure, and quality of life. However, the quality of many studies is moderate at best, and larger, well-designed trials are needed to conclusively determine the effectiveness of these interventions.

Mind-Body Practices

Mind-body practices, such as mindfulness-based stress reduction (MBSR), have been examined for their potential benefits in diabetes management. Several small studies suggest that MBSR can lead to reductions in stress and depressive symptoms, and potentially even improvements in blood glucose control in individuals with diabetes. However, these findings are preliminary and should be confirmed in larger, more rigorous studies. For an illustrative example, consider Jane, a woman with type 2 diabetes who is interested in using mindfulness practices to manage her stress levels. She has read about a study in which participants with type 2 diabetes who underwent an 8-week mindfulness-based cognitive therapy program showed improvements in depressive symptoms and blood glucose control compared to a control group. However, Jane's healthcare provider explains that while the study's findings are promising, they should be interpreted with caution due to the small sample size and lack of long-term follow-up.

The evidence base for complementary and alternative therapies in diabetes management is continually evolving, with new research published regularly. While some therapies have shown potential benefits in early-stage research, they should not be used as a replacement for conventional treatments unless their effectiveness and safety have been conclusively demonstrated in large, well-conducted trials. Patients interested in trying complementary or alternative therapies should discuss this with their healthcare provider to ensure they have the most up-to-date information and can make an informed decision. The integration of these therapies into a diabetes management plan should be done with careful monitoring to assess their impact and safety. Evidence-based complementary and alternative therapies can offer additional strategies for managing diabetes, enhancing well-being, and improving quality of life when used responsibly and under the guidance of a healthcare provider.

Risks and Precautions

Using complementary and alternative therapies can be an appealing option for people living with diabetes, primarily due to the perception that "natural" or "holistic" treatments carry fewer risks than conventional medications. However, while these therapies can complement the conventional diabetes management plan, they also present unique risks and considerations that must be carefully evaluated. This chapter will illuminate these risks and precautions, in the hope of enabling readers to make informed decisions about their health. Firstly, not all complementary and alternative therapies are created equal.

Many dietary supplements, for instance, are not regulated to the same extent as prescription medications in the United States. The Food and Drug Administration (FDA) does not rigorously scrutinize these products for safety and efficacy before they reach the market. As a result, the quality and composition of dietary supplements can vary widely between different brands and even between different batches of the same brand. Certain products might contain contaminants or not contain the advertised ingredients at all. Moreover, just because a therapy is natural does not mean it's safe. For example, bitter melon is a traditional plant-based remedy used in some cultures to treat diabetes.

While it can lower blood glucose levels, consuming it in large amounts or for a long time may cause abdominal pain, diarrhea, and potentially harmful drops in blood sugar levels. The key lesson here is that natural does not equate to safe or suitable for everyone. Complementary and alternative therapies can also interact with conventional diabetes medications. For example, ginseng, a common herbal supplement, may affect blood sugar levels and could potentially interact with insulin or other diabetes drugs, leading to low blood sugar (hypoglycemia). It's crucial that individuals disclose all supplements and alternative therapies they are using to their healthcare providers to avoid harmful interactions. Consider the case of John, a person living with type 2 diabetes. John heard about the potential benefits of a certain herbal supplement and decided to try it without consulting his doctor. After a few weeks, he started experiencing unexplained hypoglycemic episodes. It was only after a detailed conversation with his healthcare provider that they determined the supplement was interacting with his prescription diabetes medication, causing these episodes.

Another potential risk is the delay or avoidance of proven treatments. Some people might choose to use alternative therapies instead of following their prescribed diabetes management plan, which can lead to poorly controlled blood glucose and a higher risk of complications. It's essential to remember that while some complementary therapies can enhance conventional diabetes treatment, they should not replace proven strategies for managing this condition. Safety should always be the top priority when considering the use of complementary and alternative therapies for diabetes management.

It's paramount to do thorough research and consult a healthcare provider before starting any new treatment. Always remember that these therapies are intended to complement, not replace, conventional diabetes care. Using them safely involves being well-informed about their potential risks, discussing their use with healthcare providers, and carefully monitoring their effects. By taking these precautions, individuals can utilize complementary and alternative therapies responsibly, making the most of their potential benefits while minimizing the risks.

Chapter 14: Coping with Diabetes

Dealing with the Emotional Impact of Diabetes

Diabetes, being a lifelong condition, can exert a significant emotional toll on individuals. A diagnosis triggers a cascade of feelings, from disbelief and denial to fear, anxiety, and even depression. Each of these emotional stages is an integral part of the journey of living with diabetes, and recognizing, understanding, and managing them are crucial elements of effective diabetes care. The initial diagnosis often comes as a shock, abruptly changing a person's health trajectory. This sudden alteration in life's course can incite denial, a phase where the reality of having a chronic condition might be mentally brushed aside. However, persistent denial that inhibits appropriate disease management could lead to deleterious health outcomes. Acceptance, thus, is the first step towards successful diabetes management.

It entails a full understanding of the disease and the realization that while diabetes is a part of life, it does not define it. Moving past denial, individuals often grapple with fear, anxiety, and sadness. Fear and anxiety arise from thoughts of managing the disease, potential complications, and navigating the labyrinth of lifestyle modifications. There's a mourning process, too, as one grieves the loss of a time when health concerns didn't permeate everyday life. Concerns about being a burden to loved ones, and the social ramifications such as injecting insulin at public places or negotiating social gatherings with dietary restrictions can add to the emotional strain. Remember, these feelings are a normal part of the process and acknowledging them is an essential step towards managing them effectively. Among the panoply of emotions, depression is a significant concern for people with diabetes.

The relentless nature of diabetes, the constant vigilance it requires, and the pressure of adhering to dietary and medication regimens can trigger feelings of helplessness and hopelessness, often manifesting as depression. It's important to underscore that professional help is readily available and seeking it is a sign of strength, not weakness. Addressing these emotional challenges requires a multipronged approach. Acceptance, as discussed earlier, is the cornerstone. It's important to understand that it's natural to experience a range of emotions, and these feelings don't signal weakness but are part of the human response to chronic conditions. Social and emotional support constitute another significant pillar. Loved ones, friends, support groups, and professional counseling can offer invaluable support.

Support groups, both in-person and online, serve as a safe space for sharing experiences, challenges, and tips for managing diabetes. Counseling services can provide customized therapeutic approaches to address mental health issues associated with diabetes. Stress management techniques also play a pivotal role in mitigating the emotional impact of diabetes. Chronic stress can complicate diabetes management by disrupting blood glucose control. Mind-body practices such as meditation, yoga, physical activities, and recreational hobbies are excellent stress busters, helping to maintain emotional equilibrium. Remember, while the emotional impact of diabetes can be daunting, it is never insurmountable. With awareness, acceptance, social support, and professional help, you can navigate these challenges and lead a fulfilling life, despite diabetes. Embracing the emotional journey is just as crucial as managing the physical symptoms, forming an integral part of holistic diabetes care.

Support Systems and Resources

When dealing with a chronic illness such as diabetes, the value of a well-established support system cannot be underestimated. It often serves as a pillar of strength, providing the emotional backing, resources, and practical help required to manage the condition effectively. Understanding how to leverage these support systems and resources is an essential aspect of living with diabetes. Professional medical support constitutes the first line of a support system.

Your healthcare team, including your primary care physician, endocrinologist, dietitian, diabetes educator, and pharmacist, plays a pivotal role in managing your diabetes. They provide the necessary medical care, devise personalized treatment plans, offer nutritional advice, and educate you about managing your condition. Regular appointments with your healthcare team ensure a continuous evaluation of your health status and adjustment of your treatment strategy as needed. Mental health professionals are a valuable part of your support system. The emotional turmoil associated with diabetes might necessitate assistance from psychologists, psychiatrists, or therapists specializing in chronic illness management.

These professionals can help you navigate feelings of anxiety, depression, or burnout that could arise from living with diabetes. They offer strategies to deal with these feelings and can provide therapies such as cognitive-behavioral therapy, which has been shown to be effective in managing the emotional challenges associated with diabetes. Support from family and friends is also indispensable. The people closest to you can provide emotional support, encouragement, and help with practical tasks. This might involve reminders for medication, assistance with dietary changes, or accompaniment to medical appointments. While it's important to maintain independence, don't hesitate to reach out to your loved ones when you need support. In addition to immediate friends and family, support groups, both online and in person, are valuable resources. These groups bring together people dealing with similar challenges, creating a safe space to share experiences, advice, and coping strategies.

Sharing experiences and advice with others who are on a similar journey can be very therapeutic. Digital resources, including mobile applications and websites, can offer useful tools to aid in diabetes management. Apps can help monitor blood glucose levels, track physical activity, provide dietary advice, and even offer reminders for medication. There are also educational websites and online platforms that offer a wealth of information on diabetes management. Financial support resources can also aid in managing the economic burden of diabetes. In the United States, programs like Medicaid or Medicare, and assistance from the Patient Advocate Foundation can help with the cost of medications, diabetes supplies, and medical appointments. It's worth exploring these options if you need financial support for your diabetes management. Finally, it's crucial to remember that while you may have diabetes, it doesn't define you. You have the power to manage your condition and lead a fulfilling life. Leveraging the various support systems and resources available to you can significantly aid in this process. The road to diabetes management is not walked alone, and with the right support and resources, you can successfully navigate your journey.

Living a Full and Active Life with Diabetes

Living a full and active life with diabetes is not only possible but should be the goal of every individual diagnosed with this chronic condition. Diabetes does not have to limit your ambitions, desires, or activities. Instead, it necessitates an informed approach to your daily life and habits, demanding you to be proactive about your health. An active lifestyle is essential for everyone and particularly beneficial for individuals with diabetes. Physical activity plays a crucial role in maintaining a healthy weight, improving cardiovascular health, and keeping blood glucose levels within the desired range. It's worth noting that you don't need to engage in rigorous exercise routines to stay active. Walking, swimming, cycling, or even engaging in household chores can be beneficial. Remember, any movement is better than no movement. However, before starting any new exercise regimen, it is crucial to consult your healthcare provider to tailor a program that suits your current health status and capabilities.

A well-balanced diet is also key to leading a full life with diabetes. Food choices significantly influence blood glucose levels, and therefore, understanding the impact of different food groups on your body is essential. Working with a dietitian can provide personalized meal plans and help learn about portion control, carbohydrate counting, and how to balance meals. This doesn't mean you can't enjoy your favorite foods. Rather, moderation and mindful eating become your guiding principles. Another aspect of living fully with diabetes is ensuring regular check-ups with your healthcare provider. Regular monitoring of your blood glucose levels, timely adjustment of medications, and routine screenings for potential complications are vital components of successful diabetes management. Regular medical appointments help detect any potential issues early and act promptly, preventing any long-term damage. Managing stress effectively is another essential component. Chronic stress can wreak havoc on your blood glucose levels and overall health. Developing effective coping strategies for stress – be it through mindfulness techniques, yoga, meditation, or hobbies – can significantly contribute to your overall well-being. Having diabetes also means you have an opportunity to become an advocate for your health, learning more about the condition, and sharing your knowledge with others. Many people living with diabetes have taken on advocacy roles, educating the public about the condition, contributing to scientific research, and even influencing health policy.

Lastly, remember that it's OK to have off days. Living with a chronic condition can be challenging, and there may be days when things don't go as planned. Recognize that it's a part of the journey, and it's important not to blame yourself during these times. Instead, use these experiences to learn, adapt, and continually improve your strategies for managing diabetes. Leading a full and active life with diabetes demands knowledge, self-care, support, and persistence. It requires you to take the reins of your health, steer it, and constantly learn from the experience. In the end, the aim should be not just to live with diabetes but to thrive with it.

Chapter 15: Preventing Complications

Short-term and Long-term Complications

Diabetes, a condition characterized by high blood glucose levels, if left unmanaged, can lead to both short-term and long-term complications. These complications can affect various organs and systems in the body, including the heart, blood vessels, nerves, eyes, kidneys, and skin. This chapter will provide an overview of these complications, their impacts, and the underlying mechanisms involved. Short-term complications of diabetes primarily include hypoglycemia and hyperglycemia. Hypoglycemia, or low blood sugar, can occur if blood glucose levels drop below the normal range. This can happen due to an imbalance between the amount of insulin taken, the amount of food eaten, and the level of physical activity. Symptoms of hypoglycemia can range from feeling shaky or dizzy, experiencing confusion, and in severe cases, loss of consciousness. If not treated promptly, hypoglycemia can be life-threatening. Hyperglycemia, on the other hand, refers to high blood glucose levels. This can occur when the body doesn't have enough insulin or can't use insulin effectively.

Symptoms of hyperglycemia include **frequent urination, excessive thirst, fatigue, and blurred vision.** If left untreated, hyperglycemia can lead to a dangerous condition called ketoacidosis, characterized by a build-up of acids, known as ketones, in the blood. Long-term complications of diabetes are often categorized as microvascular or macrovascular complications. Microvascular complications involve small blood vessels, impacting the eyes, kidneys, and nerves. Diabetic retinopathy, a leading cause of blindness, occurs when high blood glucose levels damage the blood vessels in the retina.

Diabetic nephropathy, or kidney disease, can lead to kidney failure and the need for dialysis or a kidney transplant. Diabetic neuropathy, or nerve damage, can lead to numbness or pain in the hands and feet and is a common cause of non-traumatic lower limb amputations. Macrovascular complications involve larger blood vessels and primarily lead to cardiovascular diseases. People with diabetes have a higher risk of developing coronary artery disease, peripheral artery disease, and stroke. High blood glucose levels over time can damage blood vessels and nerves controlling the heart, leading to heart disease and heart failure. Besides these, diabetes can also lead to other long-term complications such as gastroparesis (delayed stomach emptying), infections and skin conditions, erectile dysfunction, and complications in pregnancy. The risk of these complications increases with the duration of diabetes and the degree of blood glucose control.

However, it's important to note that the development of these complications is not inevitable. With proper management of blood glucose, blood pressure, and cholesterol levels, regular check-ups, and timely interventions, the risk of these complications can be significantly reduced. In conclusion, while diabetes can lead to various short-term and long-term complications, proper management and care can prevent or delay their onset. This highlights the importance of early diagnosis, patient education, and proactive disease management in improving the lives of individuals with diabetes.

Regular Check-ups and Tests

In the context of diabetes management, regular check-ups and tests play an essential role in monitoring the disease's progression and in taking preventative measures against potential complications. These tests provide an in-depth look into how well the body is managing blood glucose levels, the functioning of vital organs like the heart and kidneys, the health of the eyes, and the status of cholesterol and blood pressure levels. One of the foundational components of these tests is the glycated hemoglobin (HbA1c) test. This is a blood test that provides a summary of the average blood glucose levels over the past 2-3 months. The American Diabetes Association recommends that most adults with diabetes aim for an HbA1c level below 7%. This test is typically performed every 3-6 months, depending on the individual's treatment plan and how well their diabetes is being managed. Regular blood glucose testing, also known as self-monitoring of blood glucose (SMBG), is another key part of diabetes management. Individuals with diabetes use a blood glucose meter to check their blood glucose levels at different times during the day, typically before meals and at bedtime.

This helps to provide immediate information about blood glucose levels and can help guide decisions regarding food intake, physical activity, and medication. To monitor the health of the cardiovascular system, healthcare providers may recommend blood pressure checks, cholesterol tests, and possibly an electrocardiogram (ECG) to assess heart health. Blood pressure should ideally be less than 130/80 mm Hg in individuals with diabetes, and cholesterol levels should also be within recommended ranges to reduce the risk of cardiovascular disease. Kidney function tests, including the urine albumin test and the estimated glomerular filtration rate (eGFR), are crucial for early detection of diabetic kidney disease. These tests measure the amount of a protein called albumin in the urine and the kidneys' filtration rate, respectively. It is recommended that these tests are done at least once a year for individuals with diabetes. Eye examinations are also an integral part of the regular check-ups. High blood glucose levels can damage the blood vessels in the eyes, leading to diabetic retinopathy. Regular dilated eye examinations can help detect this condition early and initiate treatment to prevent vision loss.

Foot examinations should also be performed routinely, as diabetes can cause peripheral neuropathy, a condition characterized by nerve damage in the feet. This can lead to numbness, making it difficult to feel a cut or sore, which if left untreated, can lead to serious infections and possibly amputation. Aside from these, other tests may be necessary depending on an individual's specific health situation and the type of diabetes they have. For example, pregnant women with gestational diabetes or pre-existing diabetes may need additional tests to monitor their health and their baby's health. Regular check-ups and tests are thus an essential part of diabetes management, providing valuable information to guide treatment decisions, monitor disease progression, and initiate early interventions for potential complications. Regular healthcare visits also provide an opportunity for individuals with diabetes to discuss any concerns or issues they may have, ensuring that their treatment plan is tailored to their specific needs and circumstances.

Steps to Prevent Complications

Managing diabetes effectively requires a comprehensive, proactive approach aimed at minimizing the risk of short-term and long-term complications. While regular medical check-ups and tests are crucial in this endeavor, they form just one part of the larger strategy. The prevention of complications largely rests on maintaining good glycemic control, following a balanced diet, engaging in regular physical activity, adhering to medication regimens, and embracing lifestyle modifications that support overall well-being. Maintaining optimal blood glucose levels is the cornerstone of diabetes management. This can be achieved through regular self-monitoring of blood glucose levels, following the prescribed medication regimen, whether that includes insulin or oral hypoglycemic agents, and adjusting these medications as necessary in consultation with healthcare professionals. Dietary management plays an indispensable role in diabetes control and complication prevention. A diet rich in whole grains, lean proteins, fruits, vegetables, and low-fat dairy products, while limiting refined carbohydrates, sugars, and saturated fats, helps in maintaining steady blood glucose levels and a healthy body weight.

Collaborating with a dietitian can provide individualized meal plans that cater to personal preferences, nutritional needs, and the specific requirements of diabetes management. Regular physical activity is another critical component of diabetes management. The American Diabetes Association recommends at least 150 minutes of moderate-intensity aerobic activity per week, along with resistance training exercises at least twice a week. Physical activity aids in maintaining a healthy weight, improving insulin sensitivity, reducing cardiovascular risk, and promoting overall health. Adherence to prescribed medication is fundamental to preventing complications.

Medications for diabetes, whether oral or injectable, are designed to maintain blood glucose levels within the target range set by healthcare providers. Concurrently, medications may also be needed for related conditions like hypertension and dyslipidemia, both of which are common in people with diabetes and contribute to the risk of cardiovascular complications. Regular foot care is crucial to prevent diabetic foot complications, which can potentially lead to amputation.

This includes daily inspection of feet for any cuts, blisters, or sores, regular washing and drying, wearing comfortable shoes and socks, and seeking prompt medical attention for any foot-related issues. Routine eye and dental check-ups are essential as diabetes can lead to complications like retinopathy and gum diseases. Regular examinations help in early detection and treatment of these issues. Quit smoking and moderating alcohol intake are vital lifestyle changes for individuals with diabetes. Smoking worsens the effect of diabetes on the blood vessels and can accelerate the development of complications, while excessive alcohol can lead to unpredictable changes in blood glucose levels. Regular monitoring and management of blood pressure and cholesterol levels are also important. High blood pressure and abnormal lipid levels significantly increase the risk of cardiovascular complications in individuals with diabetes.

Lastly, it's essential to manage stress effectively as it can directly impact blood glucose levels. Stress management techniques such as mindfulness, yoga, meditation, or simply engaging in enjoyable activities can help maintain mental health and improve overall diabetes management. In conclusion, preventing complications in diabetes is a multidimensional approach that extends beyond medication and involves a holistic consideration of diet, physical activity, lifestyle modifications, and consistent self-care. Individualized care plans, designed in consultation with healthcare professionals, can guide individuals with diabetes in managing their condition and minimizing the risk of complications. The active participation of the individual in their care, coupled with the support from their healthcare team and loved ones, is vital in successfully preventing diabetes-related complications.

General Questions about Diabetes

Understanding diabetes necessitates an exploration of numerous aspects, from its fundamental nature to its potential implications. This quest for knowledge often takes the form of myriad questions that those newly diagnosed with diabetes, their caregivers, or even the general public might have about this condition. This section aims to provide comprehensive and clear answers to some of these commonly asked questions.

Firstly, one might inquire: What exactly is diabetes?

To put it simply, diabetes is a chronic medical condition characterized by an increased level of glucose (sugar) in the blood. It occurs due to the body's inability to produce sufficient insulin, as in Type 1 diabetes, or due to the body's inability to effectively use the insulin it produces, known as insulin resistance, as in Type 2 diabetes. Insulin is a hormone produced by the pancreas that regulates blood sugar levels, and any disruption in its production or function can lead to hyperglycemia, or high blood sugar. A frequently asked question pertains to the cause of diabetes. While the exact cause differs based on the type of diabetes, it's primarily a combination of genetic, environmental, and lifestyle factors. In Type 1 diabetes, an autoimmune reaction where the body's immune system attacks its insulin-producing cells in the pancreas is often responsible. In contrast, Type 2 diabetes is commonly associated with obesity, physical inactivity, poor diet, and older age.

Another question often posed is: Can diabetes be cured? Currently, there is no known cure for diabetes. However, the condition can be effectively managed with a combination of dietary modifications, physical activity, medications, and in some cases, insulin therapy. By managing their condition effectively, individuals with diabetes can lead a healthy and active life. People often wonder: What are the signs and symptoms of diabetes? Classic symptoms include frequent urination, excessive thirst, increased hunger, unexplained weight loss, tiredness, blurred vision, and slow-healing wounds. However, it's important to note that symptoms can vary from person to person, and sometimes, particularly in the early stages of Type 2 diabetes, symptoms might not be apparent. Another common query is: How is diabetes diagnosed? Diabetes is diagnosed through blood tests that measure the level of glucose in your blood. These may include a fasting plasma glucose test, an oral glucose tolerance test, or a hemoglobin A1C test. The results of these tests, in conjunction with symptoms and medical history, help in diagnosing the condition.

A critical question is: What complications can arise from diabetes? If not well-managed, diabetes can lead to various complications affecting the heart, kidneys, eyes, nerves, and feet. These include cardiovascular disease, kidney disease, retinopathy, neuropathy, and foot ulcers. The difference between Type 1 and Type 2 diabetes often sparks interest. While both are characterized by high blood glucose levels, they differ in their cause, onset, management, and sometimes, the severity of complications. Type 1 diabetes, often diagnosed in childhood, is caused by an autoimmune response, and individuals require insulin therapy. In contrast, Type 2 diabetes is more common, typically develops in adults, and is often associated with lifestyle factors. Management usually starts with diet and exercise, but can also require oral medications or insulin over time.

One important question to address is: Can diabetes be prevented? While you can't prevent Type 1 diabetes, lifestyle modifications can significantly reduce the risk of developing Type 2 diabetes. These include maintaining a healthy weight, regular physical activity, a balanced diet, regular check-ups, and avoiding smoking and excessive alcohol. Finally, living with diabetes is a common concern. It involves regular monitoring of blood sugar levels, taking prescribed medications, maintaining a healthy lifestyle, regular check-ups, and managing stress. With appropriate management, individuals with diabetes can lead full, healthy, and active lives.

Food and Diet Questions

When discussing diabetes, an essential aspect that frequently arises is the impact of diet and food choices on the management of this condition. The right dietary choices can significantly aid in maintaining blood glucose levels within a healthy range, preventing or managing weight issues, and minimizing the risk of diabetes-related complications. In this section, we address some common food and diet-related questions often posed by those dealing with diabetes. A recurrent question is: What foods should I avoid if I have diabetes? Foods with high sugar content such as sugary drinks, sweets, and desserts, as well as high-fat foods like fast food, are generally not recommended for people with diabetes. These foods can cause blood glucose levels to spike, lead to weight gain, and increase the risk of other health conditions. Additionally, processed foods high in sodium should be limited to avoid hypertension, a common complication in those with diabetes. Can a person with diabetes eat fruits? Yes, individuals with diabetes can and should eat fruits. Fruits are packed with vitamins, minerals, and fiber.

However, they also contain carbohydrates and natural sugars, so portion control is key. Consuming fruits along with a source of protein, like nuts or cheese, can slow the digestion of the sugar and prevent spikes in blood glucose levels. A frequently asked question is: How can I eat carbohydrates safely with diabetes? Carbohydrates directly impact blood sugar levels more than other nutrients. However, not all carbohydrates affect blood glucose in the same way. Complex carbohydrates, found in whole grains, legumes, and vegetables, are broken down more slowly and lead to a gradual rise in blood sugar levels. These are the best choices for individuals with diabetes. It is crucial to monitor portion sizes and utilize carbohydrate counting or the glycemic index to guide safe consumption of carbohydrates.

Many wonder: Is sugar completely off-limits for people with diabetes? Not necessarily. While limiting sugar intake is important for managing diabetes, it doesn't mean that people with diabetes cannot ever consume sugar. Small amounts can be included as part of a balanced diet.

When consuming foods with added sugars, it is vital to account for these carbohydrates in your total carbohydrate count for the day. Another common query is: Are artificial sweeteners safe for people with diabetes? Artificial sweeteners can be a safe sugar alternative for those with diabetes, as they don't raise blood sugar levels. However, they should still be used in moderation, as some studies suggest that excessive consumption might have negative health effects. What dietary changes can help manage diabetes? A balanced diet rich in lean proteins, healthy fats, fruits, vegetables, and whole grains can help manage blood glucose levels. Regular meal timings and portion control are also crucial aspects of dietary management. People with diabetes can benefit from personalized nutritional advice from a registered dietitian.

Lastly, Does obesity play a role in diabetes? Obesity is a significant risk factor for developing type 2 diabetes. Excess body fat, particularly around the abdomen, is linked to insulin resistance, a key characteristic of type 2 diabetes. Therefore, maintaining a healthy weight through diet and regular physical activity can significantly reduce the risk of developing this condition. In conclusion, while there are certain considerations to keep in mind, having diabetes does not mean resigning oneself to a bland and restrictive diet. It's about making healthier choices, practicing portion control, and maintaining a balance of nutrients. This can lead to better diabetes management and a healthier overall life.

Exercise Questions

Physical activity plays a crucial role in the management of diabetes. Exercise helps control blood glucose levels, reduce body weight, increase insulin sensitivity, and improve cardiovascular health. However, there are often many questions related to exercise for individuals living with diabetes. This section aims to provide detailed answers to some of these common queries. One frequent question is: How much exercise should a person with diabetes do? The American Diabetes Association recommends at least 150 minutes of moderate-intensity aerobic exercise spread out over at least three days during the week, with no more than two consecutive days between exercises. Additionally, strength training exercises should be performed at least twice a week. These recommendations may vary based on individual health conditions, so it's essential to consult with a healthcare provider before starting any new exercise routine. Another common question is: What types of exercises are best for people with diabetes? Both aerobic and resistance training exercises are beneficial. Aerobic exercises such as brisk walking, cycling, or swimming help improve cardiovascular health and control blood glucose.

Resistance or strength training exercises like weight lifting or yoga help build muscle mass, which can improve metabolic rate and insulin sensitivity. Are there any precautions to be taken while exercising? Yes, individuals with diabetes need to take specific precautions while exercising. It's crucial to monitor blood glucose levels before, during, and after exercise as physical activity can cause fluctuations in these levels. This is particularly important for individuals who take insulin or other glucose-lowering medications that can cause hypoglycemia. Wearing proper footwear to prevent foot injuries, staying well-hydrated, and avoiding exercising in extreme temperatures are other necessary precautions. Can physical activity lead to low blood sugar? Exercise increases the body's insulin sensitivity, meaning that your cells are better able to use any available insulin to absorb glucose during and after activity. If you take insulin or a sulfonylurea, this increased sensitivity can lead to hypoglycemia (low blood sugar). If you're at risk for hypoglycemia, it's advisable to eat a small snack before exercising.

Many ask: How does exercise benefit individuals with diabetes? Exercise provides numerous health benefits. It helps lower blood glucose levels, reduces the risk of heart disease, aids in weight management, improves insulin sensitivity, reduces stress, and enhances overall well-being. Lastly, How can I motivate myself to stay active? It's important to choose activities that you enjoy to maintain motivation. Setting achievable goals, tracking your progress, and working with a personal trainer or enrolling in an exercise class can also help. In addition, involving family and friends can make exercising more enjoyable and encourage you to stay active. The value of exercise in managing diabetes cannot be overstated. By integrating regular physical activity into their daily routine, individuals with diabetes can significantly improve their health and quality of life. However, it's important to remember that everyone's response to exercise is unique, especially for individuals with diabetes. Therefore, a personalized approach under the guidance of a healthcare professional is necessary to ensure safety and effectiveness.

Medication and Insulin Questions

The proper use of medication and insulin is essential in managing diabetes. The array of questions that patients often have regarding these treatments underscores the need for accurate and detailed responses. One frequently asked question is: What are the different types of diabetes medications available? For individuals with type 2 diabetes, several classes of oral medications are available, including metformin, sulfonylureas, DPP-4 inhibitors, SGLT2 inhibitors, and thiazolidinediones. Each class of drugs works differently to lower blood glucose levels. For type 1 diabetes and some cases of type 2 diabetes, insulin is the primary treatment. Insulin types vary in how fast they start to work and how long they last in your body. These include rapid-acting, short-acting, intermediate-acting, and long-acting insulin. Another common inquiry is: When should insulin be taken? The timing of insulin administration depends on the type of insulin prescribed. For instance, rapid-acting insulin is typically taken just before, during, or after meals, while long-acting insulin is generally taken once or twice a day, regardless of meals.

It's important to follow the healthcare provider's specific instructions regarding insulin administration to maintain optimal blood glucose control. What are the side effects of diabetes medication and insulin? Side effects vary depending on the medication. Common side effects of many oral diabetes medications include upset stomach, fatigue, and dizziness. Insulin therapy can lead to hypoglycemia (low blood sugar), weight gain, and in some cases, skin reactions at the injection site. The healthcare provider will discuss the potential side effects of each medication or insulin type before starting the treatment. Patients often ask: Can I stop taking my medication or insulin if my blood sugar levels are consistently within the target range? Diabetes is a chronic condition, and even if blood glucose levels are within the target range, it's generally due to the effects of the ongoing medication or insulin regimen. Stopping medication or insulin can lead to a rapid increase in blood glucose levels. Any changes to the treatment plan should always be made in consultation with the healthcare provider. Another crucial question is: What should I do if I forget to take my medication or administer insulin? If a dose is missed, it's typically advised not to double the next dose. Instead, the person should take the missed dose as soon as remembered, provided it's not too close to the timing of the next scheduled dose. However, specific recommendations may vary based on the medication and individual circumstances, so it's vital to discuss this with the healthcare provider.

How should insulin be stored? Insulin should be stored in the refrigerator until the vial or pen is opened. Once opened, it can be kept at room temperature for about a month. Insulin should not be exposed to extreme temperatures, and any insulin that appears discolored or contains particles should not be used. Managing diabetes with medication and insulin can be complex, and understanding the nature of these treatments is fundamental to achieving effective blood glucose control. In all cases, patients should maintain open communication with their healthcare provider to ensure they are using their medications appropriately and address any concerns or questions promptly.

DID YOU LIKE THIS BOOK?

To provide the best quality cases to customers, we **would love to hear your thoughts and opinions on this book.**

Your feedback will help me in continually improving my current and future books. I genuinely hope that your experience with my product was positive and memorable!

TO DO SO, I WOULD ENCOURAGE YOU TO <u>LEAVE A HONEST REVIEW ON AMAZON</u>.

<u>**THANK YOU IN ADVANCE FOR YOUR VALUABLE FEEDBACK**</u>!

Made in United States
North Haven, CT
22 July 2023

39402190R00059